# Irish Pub Cookbook

By Brad Hoskinson

Copyright 2025 By Brad Hoskinson. All rights reserved.

No part of this book may be reproduced in any form or by any electronic or mechanical means, including information storage and retrieval systems, without written permission from the author, except for the use of brief quotations in a book review.

# Table of Contents

Irish Potato Skins with Cheese & Bacon .................................................. 7

Guinness Beer Cheese Dip ........................................................................ 8

Irish Sausage Rolls .................................................................................... 9

Dublin-Style Crab Cakes ........................................................................ 10

Colcannon Potato Bites .......................................................................... 11

Boxty with Smoked Salmon ................................................................... 12

Reuben Egg Rolls ................................................................................... 13

Irish Nachos (Potato-Based) .................................................................. 14

Black Pudding Scotch Eggs ................................................................... 15

Cheddar & Stout Fondue ........................................................................ 16

Mussels in Irish Cider ............................................................................. 17

Corned Beef Sliders ................................................................................ 18

Whiskey-Glazed Chicken Wings ........................................................... 19

Dublin Bay Prawn Cocktail .................................................................... 20

Irish Soda Bread with Honey Butter ...................................................... 21

Stout-Braised Onion Dip ........................................................................ 22

Blarney Cheese Sticks ............................................................................ 23

Caraway Seed Crackers with Irish Cheddar .......................................... 24

Traditional Irish Oatcakes ...................................................................... 25

Smoked Mackerel Pâté ........................................................................... 26

Irish Leek & Potato Soup ....................................................................... 27

Guinness & Onion Soup ......................................................................... 28

Dublin Coddle Soup ............................................................................... 29

Smoked Salmon & Potato Salad ............................................................ 30

Irish Whiskey Tomato Soup .................................................................. 31

Corned Beef & Cabbage Salad ............................................................... 32

Creamy Parsnip Soup ............................................................................. 33

| | |
|---|---|
| Irish Coleslaw | 34 |
| Beetroot & Goat Cheese Salad | 35 |
| Mussel Chowder | 36 |
| Classic Irish Stew | 37 |
| Beef & Guinness Pie | 38 |
| Shepherd's Pie | 40 |
| Cottage Pie | 41 |
| Bangers & Mash with Onion Gravy | 42 |
| Dublin Coddle | 43 |
| Corned Beef & Cabbage | 44 |
| Stout-Braised Short Ribs | 45 |
| Boxty with Beef & Stout Sauce | 46 |
| Irish Whiskey Glazed Salmon | 47 |
| Irish Lamb Chops with Garlic Butter | 48 |
| Guinness-Braised Brisket | 49 |
| Chicken & Leek Pie | 50 |
| Steak & Ale Pie | 52 |
| Traditional Fish & Chips | 53 |
| Beer-Battered Cod | 54 |
| Smoked Haddock Chowder | 55 |
| Irish Pork Belly with Apple Sauce | 56 |
| Seafood Pie | 57 |
| Bacon & Cabbage with Parsley Sauce | 58 |
| Champ (Mashed Potatoes with Scallions) | 60 |
| Roasted Root Vegetables with Honey & Thyme | 61 |
| Boxty (Irish Potato Pancakes) | 62 |
| Buttered Cabbage | 63 |
| Parsnip & Potato Gratin | 64 |

|  |  |
|---|---|
| Irish Brown Bread | 65 |
| Guinness-Braised Onions | 66 |
| Traditional Soda Bread | 67 |
| Carrot & Parsnip Mash | 68 |
| Classic Reuben Sandwich | 69 |
| Irish Breakfast Sandwich | 70 |
| Corned Beef & Swiss Melt | 71 |
| Stout-Marinated Steak Sandwich | 72 |
| Dublin-Style Chicken Club | 73 |
| Guinness BBQ Pulled Pork Sandwich | 74 |
| Smoked Salmon & Cream Cheese Bagel | 75 |
| Battered Fish Wrap with Tartar Sauce | 76 |
| Irish Cheddar & Apple Grilled Cheese | 77 |
| Black Pudding Breakfast Wrap | 78 |
| Guinness Chocolate Cake | 79 |
| Bailey's Cheesecake | 81 |
| Sticky Toffee Pudding | 83 |
| Irish Apple Cake | 85 |
| Whiskey Bread Pudding | 87 |
| Porter Chocolate Mousse | 89 |
| Irish Cream Brownies | 90 |
| Barmbrack (Irish Fruitcake) | 91 |
| Chocolate Stout Truffles | 93 |
| Shamrock Sugar Cookies | 94 |
| Raspberry & White Chocolate Scones | 95 |
| Irish Oat Flapjacks | 97 |
| Bailey's Tiramisu | 98 |
| Method: | 98 |

Irish Whiskey Caramel Tart ................................................................................. 99
Honey & Oat Ice Cream ..................................................................................... 100
Butterscotch & Stout Pudding ............................................................................ 101
Irish Coffee Cake ................................................................................................ 102
Whiskey Chocolate Fudge .................................................................................. 104
Guinness Float .................................................................................................... 105
Classic Irish Coffee ............................................................................................. 106
Bailey's Irish Cream Latte .................................................................................. 107
Guinness & Blackcurrant .................................................................................... 108
Irish Mule (Whiskey & Ginger Beer) ................................................................. 109
Black Velvet (Guinness & Champagne) ............................................................. 110
Dublin Sour (Whiskey & Lemon) ....................................................................... 111
Shamrock Shake (Alcoholic or Non-Alcoholic) ................................................. 112
Bailey's Espresso Martini ................................................................................... 113
Irish Hot Toddy ................................................................................................... 114
Stout & Irish Cream Milkshake .......................................................................... 115
Green Beer .......................................................................................................... 116

# Irish Potato Skins with Cheese & Bacon

These crispy and cheesy potato skins are a classic Irish appetizer. Loaded with gooey cheese, crispy bacon, and a dollop of sour cream, they are a perfect finger food for any celebration.

Prep Time: 15 minutes Cook Time: 35 minutes

## Ingredients:

- ✓ 4 large russet potatoes
- ✓ 1 cup shredded cheddar cheese
- ✓ 6 slices bacon, cooked and crumbled
- ✓ ½ cup sour cream
- ✓ 2 tablespoons chopped green onions
- ✓ 2 tablespoons olive oil
- ✓ Salt and pepper to taste

## Method:

1. Preheat the oven to 400°F (200°C).
2. Wash and scrub the potatoes, then prick them with a fork. Bake them on a baking sheet for 35 minutes or until tender.
3. Let the potatoes cool slightly, then cut them in half and scoop out the insides, leaving about ¼ inch of potato flesh.
4. Brush the potato skins with olive oil and season with salt and pepper. Bake for 10-15 minutes until crispy.
5. Remove the skins from the oven and stuff them with shredded cheese and crumbled bacon. Return them to the oven for 5-7 minutes, until the cheese melts.
6. Top with a dollop of sour cream and chopped green onions before serving.

# Guinness Beer Cheese Dip

This rich, creamy dip combines the deep flavors of Guinness beer with melted cheese. It's perfect for pairing with pretzels, crackers, or veggies.

Prep Time: 10 minutes Cook Time: 10 minutes

## Ingredients:

- ✓ 1 cup Guinness beer
- ✓ 1 tablespoon butter
- ✓ 1 tablespoon flour
- ✓ 1 cup sharp cheddar cheese, grated
- ✓ ½ cup cream cheese, softened
- ✓ Salt and pepper to taste
- ✓ 1 teaspoon mustard powder (optional)

## Method:

1. In a medium saucepan, melt the butter over medium heat.
2. Add the flour and whisk continuously for 1-2 minutes to form a roux.
3. Gradually pour in the Guinness beer, whisking constantly to avoid lumps.
4. Add the cream cheese and cheddar cheese, stirring until melted and smooth.
5. Season with salt, pepper, and mustard powder if using.
6. Serve hot with pretzels, crackers, or vegetable sticks.

# Irish Sausage Rolls

Irish sausage rolls are a savory, handheld snack made with Irish sausage wrapped in flaky puff pastry. They're great for parties, picnics, or a cozy evening snack.

Prep Time: 20 minutes Cook Time: 25 minutes

## Ingredients:

- ✓ 1 pound Irish sausage (or any preferred sausage)
- ✓ 1 sheet puff pastry
- ✓ 1 egg, beaten
- ✓ Salt and pepper to taste
- ✓ 1 teaspoon dried thyme (optional)

## Method:

1. Preheat the oven to 375°F (190°C).
2. Roll out the puff pastry sheet and cut it into 3-4 rectangular strips.
3. Remove the sausage from its casing and place the sausage meat in the center of each pastry strip.
4. Roll up the pastry around the sausage and press the seams to seal.
5. Brush the pastry rolls with the beaten egg and season with salt, pepper, and thyme.
6. Place the rolls on a baking sheet lined with parchment paper and bake for 20-25 minutes, or until golden brown.
7. Serve warm.

# Dublin-Style Crab Cakes

These flavorful crab cakes are a nod to the flavors of Dublin, with a crispy golden exterior and a tender, seasoned crab filling. Perfect as an appetizer or main course.

Prep Time: 15 minutes Cook Time: 10 minutes

## Ingredients:

- 1 pound fresh crab meat
- 1 egg
- ½ cup breadcrumbs
- 2 tablespoons mayonnaise
- 1 tablespoon Dijon mustard
- 1 teaspoon Old Bay seasoning
- 1 tablespoon chopped parsley
- 1 tablespoon lemon juice
- Salt and pepper to taste
- Olive oil for frying

## Method:

1. In a bowl, combine the crab meat, egg, breadcrumbs, mayonnaise, mustard, Old Bay seasoning, parsley, and lemon juice.
2. Season with salt and pepper and mix until well combined.
3. Shape the mixture into small patties.
4. Heat olive oil in a skillet over medium heat and cook the patties for 3-4 minutes per side, or until golden brown.
5. Serve with a lemon wedge or dipping sauce.

# Colcannon Potato Bites

Colcannon is a traditional Irish dish made from mashed potatoes, cabbage, and scallions. In this version, it's transformed into crispy bites for an irresistible snack.

Prep Time: 15 minutes Cook Time: 15 minutes

## Ingredients:

- 2 cups mashed potatoes (preferably leftover)
- 1 cup cabbage, finely shredded
- 2 scallions, chopped
- 1 egg, beaten
- 1 tablespoon flour
- Salt and pepper to taste
- Olive oil for frying

## Method:

1. Mix together the mashed potatoes, cabbage, scallions, egg, flour, salt, and pepper.
2. Form the mixture into small balls or patties.
3. Heat olive oil in a frying pan over medium heat.
4. Fry the potato bites for 3-4 minutes per side, or until golden and crispy.
5. Serve hot with sour cream or your favorite dipping sauce.

# Boxty with Smoked Salmon

Boxty is a traditional Irish potato pancake, and when paired with smoked salmon, it becomes a delicious and elegant dish, perfect for breakfast or brunch.

Prep Time: 10 minutes Cook Time: 10 minutes

## Ingredients:

- 1 cup grated potatoes
- 1 cup flour
- 1 teaspoon baking powder
- 1 egg
- ½ cup buttermilk
- Salt and pepper to taste
- 4 ounces smoked salmon
- 2 tablespoons sour cream
- Fresh dill for garnish

## Method:

1. In a bowl, mix the grated potatoes, flour, baking powder, egg, buttermilk, salt, and pepper to form a batter.
2. Heat a non-stick skillet over medium heat and add a little oil.
3. Spoon the batter onto the skillet to form small pancakes and cook for 3-4 minutes per side until golden.
4. Top each boxty with smoked salmon, a dollop of sour cream, and a sprinkle of fresh dill.
5. Serve warm.

# Reuben Egg Rolls

A fun twist on the classic Reuben sandwich, these egg rolls are crispy on the outside and filled with corned beef, Swiss cheese, sauerkraut, and thousand island dressing.

Prep Time: 10 minutes Cook Time: 10 minutes

## Ingredients:

- ✓ 1 cup cooked corned beef, shredded
- ✓ 1 cup Swiss cheese, shredded
- ✓ ½ cup sauerkraut, drained
- ✓ ¼ cup thousand island dressing
- ✓ 8 egg roll wrappers
- ✓ Olive oil for frying

## Method:

1. In a bowl, mix the corned beef, Swiss cheese, sauerkraut, and thousand island dressing.
2. Place a spoonful of the mixture in the center of each egg roll wrapper and roll it up tightly.
3. Heat olive oil in a pan over medium heat and fry the egg rolls for 2-3 minutes per side, or until golden and crispy.
4. Serve with additional thousand island dressing for dipping.

# Irish Nachos (Potato-Based)

Forget the traditional tortilla chips; these Irish nachos use crispy, thinly sliced potatoes as the base, topped with cheese, bacon, and sour cream.

Prep Time: 10 minutes  Cook Time: 25 minutes

## Ingredients:

- 4 large potatoes, thinly sliced
- 1 cup shredded cheddar cheese
- 6 slices bacon, crumbled
- ¼ cup sour cream
- 2 tablespoons chopped green onions
- Salt and pepper to taste
- Olive oil for frying

## Method:

1. Preheat the oven to 375°F (190°C).
2. Arrange the sliced potatoes in a single layer on a baking sheet, drizzle with olive oil, and season with salt and pepper.
3. Bake for 20-25 minutes, flipping halfway through, until crispy.
4. Top the baked potatoes with shredded cheddar cheese and crumbled bacon, and bake for an additional 5 minutes until the cheese is melted.
5. Top with sour cream and green onions before serving.

# Black Pudding Scotch Eggs

A unique Irish twist on the classic Scotch egg, featuring black pudding alongside sausage meat and a soft-boiled egg wrapped in breadcrumbs.

Prep Time: 15 minutes Cook Time: 15 minutes

## Ingredients:

- ✓ 4 soft-boiled eggs, peeled
- ✓ 1 cup black pudding, crumbled
- ✓ ½ cup sausage meat
- ✓ 1 egg, beaten
- ✓ 1 cup breadcrumbs
- ✓ Olive oil for frying

## Method:

1. Mix the crumbled black pudding and sausage meat together.
2. Flatten the mixture into patties and wrap each soft-boiled egg with the mixture.
3. Dip each wrapped egg into the beaten egg, then coat with breadcrumbs.
4. Heat olive oil in a pan and fry the Scotch eggs for 3-4 minutes, or until golden and crispy.
5. Serve with mustard or your favorite dipping sauce.

# Cheddar & Stout Fondue

A decadent cheese fondue made with sharp cheddar and Irish stout, perfect for dipping bread, veggies, and sausages.

Prep Time: 5 minutes   Cook Time: 10 minutes

## Ingredients:

- ✓ 1 cup cheddar cheese, grated
- ✓ ½ cup Irish stout beer
- ✓ 1 tablespoon flour
- ✓ 1 tablespoon butter
- ✓ 1 teaspoon Dijon mustard
- ✓ Salt and pepper to taste

## Method:

1. In a saucepan, melt the butter over medium heat and whisk in the flour to form a roux.
2. Gradually add the stout beer, whisking to avoid lumps.
3. Stir in the grated cheddar cheese and Dijon mustard, cooking until melted and smooth.
4. Season with salt and pepper.
5. Serve warm with bread, veggies, and sausages for dipping.

# Mussels in Irish Cider

Mussels cooked in Irish cider create a rich, slightly sweet dish that's full of flavor. The combination of the cider and mussels makes for a delicious and unique seafood meal perfect for a hearty lunch or dinner.

Prep Time: 10 minutes Cook Time: 15 minutes

## Ingredients:

- ✓ 2 pounds fresh mussels, cleaned and debearded
- ✓ 1 tablespoon butter
- ✓ 1 medium onion, finely chopped
- ✓ 2 cloves garlic, minced
- ✓ 1 cup dry Irish cider
- ✓ ½ cup heavy cream
- ✓ 2 tablespoons chopped parsley
- ✓ Salt and pepper to taste

## Method:

1. In a large pot, melt the butter over medium heat.
2. Add the chopped onion and garlic, sautéing until softened (about 3-4 minutes).
3. Pour in the Irish cider, bring to a boil, and let it simmer for 2-3 minutes to reduce slightly.
4. Add the mussels to the pot and cover with a lid. Cook for 5-7 minutes, shaking the pot occasionally until the mussels have opened.
5. Stir in the heavy cream and season with salt and pepper.
6. Remove from heat and sprinkle with chopped parsley.
7. Serve the mussels with crusty bread to soak up the delicious cider broth.

# Corned Beef Sliders

These mini corned beef sliders are perfect for a party or a festive St. Patrick's Day celebration. The tender corned beef, paired with tangy mustard and melty cheese, makes for an irresistible bite.

Prep Time: 10 minutes  Cook Time: 20 minutes

## Ingredients:

- ✓ 1 pound corned beef, thinly sliced
- ✓ 8 slider buns
- ✓ 4 ounces Swiss cheese, sliced
- ✓ 2 tablespoons Dijon mustard
- ✓ 1 tablespoon butter
- ✓ ½ cup sauerkraut (optional)

## Method:

1. Preheat the oven to 350°F (175°C).
2. Slice the slider buns in half and spread Dijon mustard on the bottom half of each bun.
3. Layer the bottom halves with slices of corned beef, Swiss cheese, and sauerkraut (if using).
4. Place the tops of the buns over the filling.
5. Melt the butter and brush it over the top of each slider bun.
6. Bake the sliders for 10-12 minutes, or until the cheese is melted and the buns are golden brown.
7. Serve warm and enjoy!

# Whiskey-Glazed Chicken Wings

Whiskey-glazed chicken wings are a flavorful, sticky, and sweet treat that packs a punch. The rich whiskey sauce adds depth, while the crispy wings are perfect for game day or a casual dinner.

Prep Time: 15 minutes  Cook Time: 25 minutes

## Ingredients:

- 12 chicken wings, separated into drums and flats
- ¼ cup Irish whiskey
- 3 tablespoons brown sugar
- 2 tablespoons soy sauce
- 1 tablespoon Dijon mustard
- 1 teaspoon garlic powder
- 1 teaspoon smoked paprika
- Salt and pepper to taste
- 2 tablespoons olive oil

## Method:

1. Preheat the oven to 400°F (200°C).
2. In a small saucepan, combine the whiskey, brown sugar, soy sauce, Dijon mustard, garlic powder, smoked paprika, salt, and pepper.
3. Bring the mixture to a simmer over medium heat and cook for 5-7 minutes, until it thickens slightly.
4. Heat olive oil in a skillet over medium-high heat.
5. Season the chicken wings with salt and pepper, then fry in the skillet for 6-7 minutes per side, until golden brown and crispy.
6. Transfer the wings to a baking sheet and brush with the whiskey glaze.
7. Bake for 10 minutes, then brush with more glaze and bake for an additional 5 minutes.
8. Serve the wings with extra glaze on the side for dipping.

# Dublin Bay Prawn Cocktail

This classic seafood cocktail is perfect as an appetizer. The sweet and succulent Dublin Bay prawns are tossed in a tangy cocktail sauce and served with crisp lettuce for a refreshing start to your meal.

Prep Time: 10 minutes Cook Time: 5 minutes

## Ingredients:

- 1 pound Dublin Bay prawns, cooked and peeled
- 2 tablespoons mayonnaise
- 1 tablespoon ketchup
- 1 teaspoon Worcestershire sauce
- 1 teaspoon lemon juice
- Salt and pepper to taste
- 4 leaves of lettuce (for serving)
- Lemon wedges for garnish

## Method:

1. In a bowl, combine the mayonnaise, ketchup, Worcestershire sauce, lemon juice, salt, and pepper.
2. Toss the prawns in the sauce until evenly coated.
3. Place a lettuce leaf in each serving dish and top with the prawns.
4. Garnish with lemon wedges and serve chilled.

# Irish Soda Bread with Honey Butter

Irish soda bread is a simple, hearty bread made with baking soda instead of yeast. Served warm with honey butter, it's the perfect accompaniment to any meal, or simply enjoyed on its own.

Prep Time: 10 minutes Cook Time: 45 minutes

## Ingredients:

- ✓ 2 cups all-purpose flour
- ✓ 1 teaspoon baking soda
- ✓ 1 teaspoon salt
- ✓ 1 tablespoon sugar
- ✓ ¾ cup buttermilk
- ✓ 2 tablespoons melted butter
- ✓ For Honey Butter:
- ✓ ½ cup unsalted butter, softened
- ✓ 2 tablespoons honey

## Method:

1. Preheat the oven to 375°F (190°C).
2. In a large bowl, combine the flour, baking soda, salt, and sugar.
3. Make a well in the center and add the buttermilk and melted butter. Stir until the dough comes together.
4. Turn the dough onto a floured surface and knead it gently for 2-3 minutes.
5. Shape the dough into a round loaf and place it on a greased baking sheet.
6. Cut a deep cross on the top of the loaf with a knife.
7. Bake for 40-45 minutes, or until the bread sounds hollow when tapped on the bottom.
8. For the honey butter, mix the softened butter and honey together until smooth.
9. Serve the bread warm with a spread of honey butter.

# Stout-Braised Onion Dip

This hearty onion dip is perfect for any gathering. The stout adds a rich, malty flavor, and the caramelized onions bring out a natural sweetness. It's great for dipping chips, crackers, or veggies.

Prep Time: 10 minutes Cook Time: 25 minutes

## Ingredients:

- ✓ 2 large onions, thinly sliced
- ✓ 1 tablespoon butter
- ✓ 1 cup stout beer
- ✓ 1 cup sour cream
- ✓ ½ cup mayonnaise
- ✓ 1 teaspoon garlic powder
- ✓ Salt and pepper to taste

## Method:

1. In a skillet, melt the butter over medium heat.
2. Add the onions and cook, stirring occasionally, until the onions are caramelized (about 10 minutes).
3. Pour in the stout and cook for an additional 5-7 minutes, allowing the liquid to reduce by half.
4. In a bowl, combine the sour cream, mayonnaise, garlic powder, salt, and pepper.
5. Stir in the caramelized onions and stout mixture.
6. Serve the dip warm with chips or crackers.

# Blarney Cheese Sticks

These cheesy, crispy sticks are perfect as a snack or appetizer. With a blend of Irish cheese and a crunchy coating, they're a great addition to any party spread.

> Prep Time: 15 minutes Cook Time: 10 minutes

## Ingredients:

- 8 ounces Irish cheddar cheese, cut into sticks
- 1 egg, beaten
- 1 cup breadcrumbs
- 1 tablespoon flour
- 1 teaspoon paprika
- Salt and pepper to taste
- Olive oil for frying

## Method:

1. Coat the cheese sticks in flour, then dip them in the beaten egg.
2. Roll the cheese sticks in breadcrumbs mixed with paprika, salt, and pepper.
3. Heat olive oil in a pan over medium heat and fry the cheese sticks for 2-3 minutes, or until golden and crispy.
4. Drain on paper towels and serve immediately.

# Caraway Seed Crackers with Irish Cheddar

These homemade crackers, infused with caraway seeds, are perfect for pairing with sharp Irish cheddar. A great addition to a cheese platter or for snacking on their own.

Prep Time: 10 minutes Cook Time: 15 minutes

## Ingredients:

- 1 cup all-purpose flour
- 1 tablespoon caraway seeds
- ½ teaspoon salt
- 3 tablespoons cold butter, cubed
- ¼ cup grated Irish cheddar
- ¼ cup cold water

## Method:

1. Preheat the oven to 375°F (190°C).
2. In a food processor, pulse together the flour, caraway seeds, and salt.
3. Add the butter and pulse until the mixture resembles coarse crumbs.
4. Add the grated cheddar and pulse again.
5. Gradually add the cold water and pulse until the dough forms.
6. Roll the dough out on a floured surface and cut into shapes.
7. Place the crackers on a baking sheet and bake for 12-15 minutes, or until golden brown.
8. Serve with more Irish cheddar.

# Traditional Irish Oatcakes

These simple and wholesome oatcakes are an Irish staple. They're crisp, slightly sweet, and perfect with butter or cheese.

Prep Time: 10 minutes Cook Time: 20 minutes

## Ingredients:

- ✓ 1 cup rolled oats
- ✓ 1 cup all-purpose flour
- ✓ ½ teaspoon baking soda
- ✓ ½ teaspoon salt
- ✓ ½ cup unsalted butter, cold and cubed
- ✓ 3-4 tablespoons water

## Method:

1. Preheat the oven to 350°F (175°C).
2. In a bowl, combine the oats, flour, baking soda, and salt.
3. Add the cold butter and rub it into the dry ingredients until it resembles breadcrumbs.
4. Gradually add water to form a dough.
5. Roll out the dough and cut into rounds or squares.
6. Place the oatcakes on a baking sheet and bake for 15-20 minutes, or until golden brown.
7. Let cool before serving.

# Smoked Mackerel Pâté

This rich and smoky pâté is a wonderful spread for crackers or bread. It's quick to make and perfect for a starter or party platter.

Prep Time: 10 minutes  Cook Time: 0 minutes

## Ingredients:

- ✓ 2 smoked mackerel fillets, skin removed
- ✓ 3 ounces cream cheese
- ✓ 1 tablespoon lemon juice
- ✓ 1 teaspoon Dijon mustard
- ✓ 1 tablespoon fresh dill, chopped
- ✓ Salt and pepper to taste

## Method:

1. Flake the smoked mackerel into small pieces.
2. In a food processor, combine the mackerel, cream cheese, lemon juice, Dijon mustard, and dill.
3. Blend until smooth, then season with salt and pepper to taste.
4. Serve the pâté with crackers or fresh bread.

# Irish Leek & Potato Soup

This comforting Irish Leek & Potato Soup is a perfect blend of smooth potatoes and mild leeks. It's a hearty, satisfying soup that brings warmth on cold days. Often served with a slice of buttered soda bread, it's an Irish classic that's simple yet delicious.

Prep Time: 10 minutes Cook Time: 30 minutes

## Ingredients:

- ✓ 2 tablespoons butter
- ✓ 3 large leeks, cleaned and sliced
- ✓ 2 cloves garlic, minced
- ✓ 4 medium potatoes, peeled and diced
- ✓ 4 cups vegetable broth
- ✓ 1 cup heavy cream (optional)
- ✓ Salt and pepper to taste
- ✓ Fresh parsley, chopped for garnish

## Method:

1. In a large pot, melt the butter over medium heat.
2. Add the sliced leeks and cook until softened (about 5 minutes).
3. Add the garlic and cook for an additional minute.
4. Stir in the potatoes and vegetable broth. Bring to a boil, then lower the heat and let it simmer for 20 minutes, or until the potatoes are tender.
5. Use an immersion blender or transfer to a regular blender and blend until smooth (if you prefer a chunkier soup, blend just half of it).
6. Stir in the heavy cream (optional), and season with salt and pepper to taste.
7. Garnish with fresh parsley before serving.

# Guinness & Onion Soup

Guinness & Onion Soup is a rich, savory soup with the deep flavors of caramelized onions and the boldness of Guinness stout. The beer adds depth to the soup, making it a perfect dish for an Irish-inspired dinner.

Prep Time: 15 minutes  Cook Time: 40 minutes

## Ingredients:

- ✓ 3 tablespoons butter
- ✓ 3 large onions, thinly sliced
- ✓ 2 cloves garlic, minced
- ✓ 1 cup Guinness beer
- ✓ 4 cups beef broth
- ✓ 1 teaspoon fresh thyme leaves
- ✓ Salt and pepper to taste
- ✓ 4 slices of French baguette
- ✓ 1 cup grated Gruyère cheese

## Method:

1. In a large pot, melt butter over medium heat.
2. Add the sliced onions and cook, stirring occasionally, for 20-25 minutes, until the onions are deeply caramelized.
3. Add the garlic and cook for another minute.
4. Pour in the Guinness beer and scrape up any browned bits from the bottom of the pot.
5. Add the beef broth and thyme, then bring the soup to a boil. Reduce the heat and let it simmer for 15-20 minutes.
6. Season with salt and pepper to taste.
7. Meanwhile, toast the slices of baguette in the oven until crispy.
8. Ladle the soup into bowls, top with a toasted baguette slice, and sprinkle with grated Gruyère cheese.
9. Place the bowls under the broiler for 3-4 minutes or until the cheese is melted and bubbly. Serve hot.

# Dublin Coddle Soup

Dublin Coddle Soup is a traditional Irish dish that is hearty and comforting. Made with sausages, bacon, and vegetables, this soup is packed with flavor and perfect for a filling meal. It's the ideal dish for a cozy night in.

Prep Time: 10 minutes  Cook Time: 1 hour

## Ingredients:

- ✓ 4 Irish sausages
- ✓ 4 slices of bacon
- ✓ 1 medium onion, chopped
- ✓ 3 medium potatoes, peeled and sliced
- ✓ 2 carrots, peeled and sliced
- ✓ 4 cups chicken broth
- ✓ 1 bay leaf
- ✓ 1 teaspoon fresh thyme
- ✓ Salt and pepper to taste
- ✓ Fresh parsley, chopped for garnish

## Method:

1. In a large pot, cook the sausages and bacon over medium heat until browned. Remove and set aside.
2. In the same pot, add the chopped onion and cook until softened.
3. Cut the sausages into pieces and chop the bacon into smaller bits. Add them back into the pot with the onion.
4. Stir in the sliced potatoes and carrots, followed by the chicken broth, bay leaf, and thyme.
5. Bring to a boil, then reduce to a simmer and cook for 45 minutes, until the vegetables are tender.
6. Season with salt and pepper to taste.
7. Serve hot, garnished with fresh parsley.

# Smoked Salmon & Potato Salad

A fresh, flavorful salad featuring the smoky richness of salmon and the heartiness of potatoes. Perfect as a main course or side dish, this salad combines crisp vegetables with creamy dressing for a refreshing dish.

Prep Time: 20 minutes  Cook Time: 15 minutes

## Ingredients:

- ✓ 2 large potatoes, boiled and diced
- ✓ 4 ounces smoked salmon, flaked
- ✓ 1 small red onion, thinly sliced
- ✓ 1 tablespoon capers
- ✓ 2 tablespoons fresh dill, chopped
- ✓ 1 tablespoon olive oil
- ✓ 2 tablespoons lemon juice
- ✓ Salt and pepper to taste

## Method:

1. Boil the potatoes in salted water until tender, then drain and allow to cool slightly.
2. In a large bowl, combine the potatoes, smoked salmon, red onion, capers, and fresh dill.
3. In a small bowl, whisk together the olive oil, lemon juice, salt, and pepper.
4. Drizzle the dressing over the salad and toss gently to combine.
5. Serve chilled or at room temperature.

# Irish Whiskey Tomato Soup

This Irish Whiskey Tomato Soup brings together the rich flavors of ripe tomatoes and the warming depth of Irish whiskey. It's a perfect twist on a classic soup that's comforting and full of flavor.

Prep Time: 10 minutes Cook Time: 25 minutes

## Ingredients:

- ✓ 2 tablespoons butter
- ✓ 1 onion, chopped
- ✓ 2 cloves garlic, minced
- ✓ 1 can (28 oz) crushed tomatoes
- ✓ 1 cup vegetable broth
- ✓ ¼ cup Irish whiskey
- ✓ 1 teaspoon dried oregano
- ✓ Salt and pepper to taste
- ✓ Fresh basil, for garnish

## Method:

1. In a large pot, melt the butter over medium heat.
2. Add the chopped onion and garlic, cooking until softened (about 5 minutes).
3. Stir in the crushed tomatoes, vegetable broth, and dried oregano. Bring to a boil.
4. Reduce heat and let the soup simmer for 15 minutes.
5. Add the Irish whiskey and cook for another 5 minutes.
6. Season with salt and pepper to taste.
7. Use an immersion blender to puree the soup to your desired consistency.
8. Serve hot, garnished with fresh basil.

# Corned Beef & Cabbage Salad

A lighter twist on the traditional Irish dish, this Corned Beef & Cabbage Salad combines the savory richness of corned beef with the crunch of cabbage and a tangy dressing. It's a fresh, vibrant salad perfect for St. Patrick's Day or any day.

Prep Time: 15 minutes   Cook Time: 10 minutes

## Ingredients:

- ✓ 1 cup cooked corned beef, sliced thinly
- ✓ 2 cups shredded cabbage
- ✓ ½ cup shredded carrots
- ✓ 1 small red onion, thinly sliced
- ✓ 2 tablespoons apple cider vinegar
- ✓ 1 tablespoon Dijon mustard
- ✓ 2 tablespoons olive oil
- ✓ Salt and pepper to taste

## Method:

1. In a large bowl, combine the shredded cabbage, carrots, red onion, and corned beef.
2. In a small bowl, whisk together the apple cider vinegar, Dijon mustard, olive oil, salt, and pepper.
3. Drizzle the dressing over the salad and toss well.
4. Serve immediately or chill in the refrigerator for 30 minutes for extra flavor.

# Creamy Parsnip Soup

This creamy parsnip soup is velvety and smooth, with a natural sweetness from the parsnips. It's a comforting soup perfect for cozying up on a chilly day.

Prep Time: 10 minutes  Cook Time: 30 minutes

## Ingredients:

- ✓ 2 tablespoons butter
- ✓ 1 onion, chopped
- ✓ 4 medium parsnips, peeled and chopped
- ✓ 2 potatoes, peeled and chopped
- ✓ 4 cups vegetable broth
- ✓ 1 cup heavy cream
- ✓ Salt and pepper to taste

## Method:

1. In a large pot, melt the butter over medium heat.
2. Add the onion and cook until softened (about 5 minutes).
3. Stir in the chopped parsnips and potatoes, followed by the vegetable broth.
4. Bring the mixture to a boil, then reduce to a simmer and cook for 20 minutes, until the vegetables are tender.
5. Use an immersion blender to puree the soup until smooth.
6. Stir in the heavy cream, and season with salt and pepper to taste.
7. Serve hot, garnished with fresh herbs if desired.

# Irish Coleslaw

Irish coleslaw is a classic side dish with a tangy, creamy dressing that pairs perfectly with hearty meats and stews. Its refreshing crunch makes it a great accompaniment to any meal.

Prep Time: 15 minutes  Cook Time: 0 minutes

## Ingredients:

- ✓ 4 cups shredded cabbage
- ✓ 1 cup shredded carrots
- ✓ ½ cup mayonnaise
- ✓ 2 tablespoons apple cider vinegar
- ✓ 1 tablespoon Dijon mustard
- ✓ Salt and pepper to taste

## Method:

1. In a large bowl, combine the shredded cabbage and carrots.
2. In a small bowl, whisk together the mayonnaise, apple cider vinegar, Dijon mustard, salt, and pepper.
3. Pour the dressing over the cabbage mixture and toss to combine.
4. Chill the coleslaw in the fridge for at least 30 minutes before serving.

# Beetroot & Goat Cheese Salad

A vibrant salad with the earthy sweetness of roasted beetroot and the creamy richness of goat cheese. This salad is light yet satisfying, perfect for lunch or as a side dish.

Prep Time: 15 minutes Cook Time: 30 minutes

## Ingredients:

- 4 medium beets, roasted and sliced
- 2 cups mixed greens (arugula, spinach, etc.)
- 4 ounces goat cheese, crumbled
- ¼ cup walnuts, toasted
- 2 tablespoons balsamic vinegar
- 2 tablespoons olive oil
- Salt and pepper to taste

## Method:

1. Preheat the oven to 400°F (200°C). Wrap the beets in foil and roast for 30 minutes until tender. Peel and slice the beets.
2. In a large bowl, combine the roasted beets, mixed greens, goat cheese, and walnuts.
3. In a small bowl, whisk together the balsamic vinegar, olive oil, salt, and pepper.
4. Drizzle the dressing over the salad and toss gently to combine.
5. Serve immediately.

# Mussel Chowder

This Mussel Chowder is a rich, creamy soup that highlights the delicate flavor of fresh mussels. It's a hearty, satisfying dish that's perfect for a cozy dinner.

Prep Time: 15 minutes Cook Time: 20 minutes

## Ingredients:

- 1 tablespoon butter
- 1 small onion, chopped
- 2 cloves garlic, minced
- 2 cups potatoes, diced
- 4 cups seafood stock
- 2 cups heavy cream
- 1 pound mussels, cleaned and debearded
- Salt and pepper to taste
- Fresh parsley, chopped for garnish

## Method:

1. In a large pot, melt the butter over medium heat.
2. Add the onion and garlic and cook until softened.
3. Stir in the diced potatoes and seafood stock. Bring to a boil and then reduce to a simmer for 10 minutes.
4. Add the heavy cream and mussels. Cover and cook for 5-7 minutes until the mussels have opened.
5. Season with salt and pepper to taste.
6. Garnish with fresh parsley and serve hot.

# Classic Irish Stew

Classic Irish Stew is the epitome of comfort food. This traditional dish combines tender lamb, hearty vegetables, and rich broth to create a filling and satisfying meal. Perfect for cold evenings, it's a quintessential Irish dish that has stood the test of time.

Prep Time: 15 minutes  Cook Time: 1 hour 30 minutes

## Ingredients:

- ✓ 1.5 pounds lamb stew meat, cut into cubes
- ✓ 2 tablespoons vegetable oil
- ✓ 1 large onion, chopped
- ✓ 4 large potatoes, peeled and cut into chunks
- ✓ 3 large carrots, peeled and sliced
- ✓ 2 celery stalks, chopped
- ✓ 4 cups beef broth
- ✓ 2 tablespoons fresh parsley, chopped
- ✓ 1 teaspoon fresh thyme leaves
- ✓ Salt and pepper to taste

## Method:

1. In a large pot, heat the vegetable oil over medium heat.
2. Brown the lamb stew meat in batches until it's all browned on all sides. Remove and set aside.
3. In the same pot, add the chopped onion and cook for about 5 minutes, until softened.
4. Return the lamb to the pot, then add the potatoes, carrots, and celery.
5. Pour in the beef broth and bring the mixture to a boil.
6. Reduce the heat to low, cover, and simmer for about 1 hour, or until the lamb is tender.
7. Season with salt, pepper, and fresh thyme.
8. Garnish with fresh parsley before serving.

# Beef & Guinness Pie

Beef & Guinness Pie is a rich and hearty dish that pairs tender chunks of beef with the deep flavors of Guinness stout. Enclosed in a golden, flaky pie crust, this comforting dish is perfect for chilly nights.

Prep Time: 20 minutes Cook Time: 2 hours

## **Ingredients:**

- ✓ 2 tablespoons olive oil
- ✓ 1 pound beef stew meat, cut into cubes
- ✓ 1 large onion, chopped
- ✓ 2 carrots, peeled and chopped
- ✓ 2 cloves garlic, minced
- ✓ 2 tablespoons tomato paste
- ✓ 2 cups Guinness stout
- ✓ 2 cups beef broth
- ✓ 2 teaspoons Worcestershire sauce
- ✓ 1 teaspoon fresh thyme leaves
- ✓ 1 sheet puff pastry, thawed
- ✓ 1 egg, beaten (for egg wash)
- ✓ Salt and pepper to taste

## **Method:**

1. Heat olive oil in a large pot over medium heat. Add the beef and cook until browned on all sides. Remove the beef and set aside.
2. In the same pot, add the onion, carrots, and garlic. Cook for about 5 minutes until softened.
3. Stir in the tomato paste and cook for 2 minutes.
4. Pour in the Guinness stout, beef broth, Worcestershire sauce, and thyme. Bring to a boil, then reduce heat to low and simmer for 1 hour, until the beef is tender.
5. Preheat the oven to 400°F (200°C).
6. Roll out the puff pastry and line a pie dish with it.
7. Spoon the beef mixture into the pie crust, then cover with the remaining pastry. Trim the edges and press to seal.

8. Brush the top of the pastry with the beaten egg.
9. Bake in the preheated oven for 30-35 minutes, or until the crust is golden brown.
10. Serve hot.

# Shepherd's Pie

Shepherd's Pie is a comforting dish made with a savory ground lamb filling, topped with creamy mashed potatoes. It's a traditional Irish and British meal that's both hearty and satisfying.

Prep Time: 20 minutes Cook Time: 1 hour

## Ingredients:

- ✓ 1 tablespoon olive oil
- ✓ 1 pound ground lamb
- ✓ 1 large onion, chopped
- ✓ 2 cloves garlic, minced
- ✓ 2 large carrots, peeled and chopped
- ✓ 1 cup peas
- ✓ 1 cup beef broth
- ✓ 1 tablespoon Worcestershire sauce
- ✓ 2 tablespoons tomato paste
- ✓ 4 cups mashed potatoes (prepared in advance)
- ✓ Salt and pepper to taste

## Method:

1. Preheat the oven to 375°F (190°C).
2. In a large skillet, heat the olive oil over medium heat. Add the ground lamb and cook until browned.
3. Add the onion, garlic, and carrots to the skillet and cook for 5 minutes, until softened.
4. Stir in the peas, beef broth, Worcestershire sauce, and tomato paste. Let simmer for 10 minutes.
5. Transfer the meat mixture to a baking dish and spread evenly.
6. Top with mashed potatoes, spreading them out evenly to cover the filling.
7. Use a fork to create a texture on the top of the potatoes.
8. Bake for 25-30 minutes, until the potatoes are golden brown.
9. Serve hot.

# Cottage Pie

Cottage Pie is similar to Shepherd's Pie but uses ground beef instead of lamb. This classic dish is comforting and filled with savory beef and vegetables, topped with mashed potatoes for a satisfying meal.

Prep Time: 20 minutes Cook Time: 1 hour

## Ingredients:

- 1 tablespoon olive oil
- 1 pound ground beef
- 1 large onion, chopped
- 2 cloves garlic, minced
- 2 carrots, peeled and chopped
- 1 cup peas
- 1 cup beef broth
- 2 tablespoons tomato paste
- 4 cups mashed potatoes (prepared in advance)
- Salt and pepper to taste

## Method:

1. Preheat the oven to 375°F (190°C).
2. In a large skillet, heat olive oil over medium heat. Add the ground beef and cook until browned.
3. Add the onion, garlic, and carrots to the skillet. Cook for 5 minutes until softened.
4. Stir in the peas, beef broth, and tomato paste. Simmer for 10 minutes, until the mixture thickens.
5. Transfer the beef mixture to a baking dish and spread evenly.
6. Spread the mashed potatoes over the top of the beef mixture.
7. Bake for 25-30 minutes until the potatoes are golden brown.
8. Serve hot.

# Bangers & Mash with Onion Gravy

Bangers & Mash is a beloved British and Irish dish of sausages (bangers) and creamy mashed potatoes (mash). Paired with rich onion gravy, it's the ultimate comfort food.

Prep Time: 10 minutes Cook Time: 30 minutes

## Ingredients:

- ✓ 8 pork sausages
- ✓ 4 large potatoes, peeled and mashed
- ✓ 2 tablespoons butter
- ✓ 2 tablespoons flour
- ✓ 2 cups beef broth
- ✓ 1 large onion, sliced
- ✓ 1 tablespoon vegetable oil
- ✓ Salt and pepper to taste

## Method:

1. In a large skillet, heat the vegetable oil over medium heat. Add the sausages and cook until browned on all sides, about 10 minutes.
2. Remove the sausages from the skillet and set aside.
3. In the same skillet, add the sliced onion and cook for 5 minutes, until softened.
4. Stir in the flour and cook for 1 minute.
5. Slowly add the beef broth, stirring constantly until the gravy thickens.
6. Season with salt and pepper.
7. Serve the sausages over mashed potatoes, topped with the onion gravy.

# Dublin Coddle

Dublin Coddle is a hearty, traditional Irish dish made with sausages, bacon, and vegetables. It's a comfort food staple in Ireland, often served on cold winter days.

Prep Time: 15 minutes Cook Time: 1 hour 30 minutes

## Ingredients:

- 4 Irish sausages
- 4 slices of bacon
- 1 large onion, chopped
- 3 medium potatoes, peeled and sliced
- 2 carrots, peeled and sliced
- 4 cups chicken broth
- 1 bay leaf
- Salt and pepper to taste

## Method:

1. In a large pot, cook the sausages and bacon until browned. Remove and set aside.
2. Add the chopped onion and cook for about 5 minutes, until softened.
3. Stir in the potatoes and carrots, then return the sausages and bacon to the pot.
4. Add the chicken broth and bay leaf, bringing to a boil.
5. Reduce heat and simmer for 1 hour, until the potatoes and sausages are cooked through.
6. Season with salt and pepper before serving.

# Corned Beef & Cabbage

Corned Beef & Cabbage is a classic Irish dish, especially popular on St. Patrick's Day. The corned beef is slowly cooked with cabbage and vegetables to create a flavorful and filling meal.

Prep Time: 10 minutes  Cook Time: 2 hours

## Ingredients:

- ✓ 3 pounds corned beef brisket
- ✓ 4 large potatoes, peeled and chopped
- ✓ 4 large carrots, peeled and chopped
- ✓ 1 small head of cabbage, chopped
- ✓ 10 cups water
- ✓ 1 tablespoon mustard seeds (optional)
- ✓ 1 tablespoon black peppercorns (optional)

## Method:

1. Place the corned beef in a large pot and cover with water.
2. Bring to a boil, then reduce the heat and simmer for 1.5-2 hours, until the meat is tender.
3. Add the potatoes and carrots, cooking for 20 minutes.
4. Add the cabbage and cook for another 10 minutes.
5. Slice the corned beef and serve with the vegetables.

# Stout-Braised Short Ribs

Stout-Braised Short Ribs are slow-cooked to tender perfection, with the deep flavor of stout beer enhancing the richness of the beef. It's a dish that's perfect for cozy dinners.

Prep Time: 15 minutes Cook Time: 3 hours

## Ingredients:

- ✓ 4 beef short ribs
- ✓ 2 tablespoons olive oil
- ✓ 1 large onion, chopped
- ✓ 2 cloves garlic, minced
- ✓ 2 cups stout beer
- ✓ 1 cup beef broth
- ✓ 2 teaspoons fresh thyme
- ✓ Salt and pepper to taste

## Method:

1. Preheat the oven to 300°F (150°C).
2. Heat olive oil in a large pot over medium heat. Brown the short ribs on all sides, then remove and set aside.
3. Add the onion and garlic to the pot and cook until softened.
4. Pour in the stout beer and beef broth, scraping up any browned bits from the pot.
5. Return the short ribs to the pot, cover, and cook in the oven for 2.5-3 hours until the meat is tender.
6. Season with salt and pepper before serving.

# Boxty with Beef & Stout Sauce

Boxty is a traditional Irish potato pancake, and when paired with beef and a rich stout sauce, it becomes an irresistible meal full of comforting flavors.

Prep Time: 10 minutes Cook Time: 30 minutes

## Ingredients:

- 2 large potatoes, grated
- 1 cup all-purpose flour
- 1 teaspoon baking powder
- ½ teaspoon salt
- 1 egg
- 1 cup buttermilk
- 1 tablespoon vegetable oil
- 1 pound beef stew meat
- 1 cup stout beer
- 1 cup beef broth

## Method:

1. In a large bowl, combine the grated potatoes, flour, baking powder, and salt.
2. Beat the egg and mix it into the potato mixture with the buttermilk.
3. Heat the oil in a skillet and cook the boxty pancakes for about 3-4 minutes per side until golden.
4. For the beef, cook the stew meat in a separate pan until browned. Add stout beer and beef broth, simmering until the sauce thickens.
5. Serve the boxty pancakes topped with the beef and stout sauce.

# Irish Whiskey Glazed Salmon

This Irish Whiskey Glazed Salmon combines the delicate flavor of salmon with a sweet and savory whiskey glaze. It's an elegant and flavorful dish perfect for a special occasion.

Prep Time: 10 minutes Cook Time: 15 minutes

## Ingredients:

- 4 salmon fillets
- 2 tablespoons Irish whiskey
- 2 tablespoons brown sugar
- 1 tablespoon Dijon mustard
- 1 tablespoon soy sauce
- 1 teaspoon lemon juice
- Salt and pepper to taste

## Method:

1. In a small bowl, whisk together the Irish whiskey, brown sugar, Dijon mustard, soy sauce, and lemon juice.
2. Preheat a grill or skillet over medium heat.
3. Season the salmon fillets with salt and pepper.
4. Brush the whiskey glaze over the salmon fillets and cook for 4-5 minutes per side, until the salmon is cooked through.
5. Serve immediately with your choice of sides.

# Irish Lamb Chops with Garlic Butter

Irish Lamb Chops with Garlic Butter is a succulent dish that highlights the rich flavors of tender lamb, enhanced with a fragrant garlic butter sauce. The simplicity of the ingredients allows the lamb's natural flavor to shine through, making this a perfect dish for a special occasion.

Prep Time: 10 minutes Cook Time: 15 minutes

## Ingredients:

- ✓ 8 lamb chops
- ✓ 2 tablespoons olive oil
- ✓ Salt and pepper to taste
- ✓ 4 tablespoons butter
- ✓ 3 cloves garlic, minced
- ✓ 1 teaspoon fresh rosemary, chopped
- ✓ 1 teaspoon fresh thyme, chopped
- ✓ 1 tablespoon lemon juice

## Method:

1. Preheat a grill or skillet over medium-high heat.
2. Rub the lamb chops with olive oil and season with salt and pepper.
3. Cook the lamb chops for about 3-4 minutes per side for medium-rare, or longer for your desired doneness.
4. While the lamb cooks, melt butter in a small pan over low heat. Add the garlic, rosemary, and thyme, cooking for about 1 minute until fragrant.
5. Drizzle the garlic butter over the lamb chops and squeeze fresh lemon juice on top.
6. Serve immediately with your favorite side dishes.

# Guinness-Braised Brisket

Guinness-Braised Brisket is a hearty dish where tender beef brisket is slowly cooked in a rich Guinness stout. The flavors of the beer infuse into the meat, making it incredibly flavorful and juicy. This dish is perfect for a family dinner or a special gathering.

Prep Time: 15 minutes Cook Time: 3 hours

## Ingredients:

- 3-4 pounds beef brisket
- 2 tablespoons olive oil
- 1 large onion, chopped
- 2 cloves garlic, minced
- 2 cups Guinness stout
- 2 cups beef broth
- 2 tablespoons brown sugar
- 1 tablespoon Worcestershire sauce
- 2 teaspoons fresh thyme leaves
- Salt and pepper to taste

## Method:

1. Preheat the oven to 300°F (150°C).
2. Heat olive oil in a large oven-safe pot over medium-high heat. Brown the brisket on all sides and set it aside.
3. Add the chopped onion and garlic to the pot, cooking for 5 minutes until softened.
4. Stir in the Guinness stout, beef broth, brown sugar, Worcestershire sauce, and thyme. Bring to a simmer.
5. Return the brisket to the pot, ensuring it is mostly submerged in the liquid. Cover and place in the oven.
6. Braise for 2.5 to 3 hours, basting occasionally, until the brisket is tender and easily pulls apart.
7. Remove the brisket from the pot and let it rest before slicing.
8. Serve with the braising liquid and your favorite side dishes.

# Chicken & Leek Pie

Chicken & Leek Pie is a creamy and comforting dish filled with tender chicken and leeks, all encased in a flaky, buttery pie crust. It's the perfect dish to enjoy on a cozy evening or to impress guests at a dinner party.

Prep Time: 20 minutes  Cook Time: 40 minutes

## Ingredients:

- 2 tablespoons butter
- 2 chicken breasts, diced
- 2 leeks, cleaned and sliced
- 2 cloves garlic, minced
- 1 cup chicken broth
- 1 cup heavy cream
- 1 tablespoon flour
- 1 teaspoon thyme leaves
- 1 sheet puff pastry
- Salt and pepper to taste
- 1 egg, beaten (for egg wash)

## Method:

1. Preheat the oven to 375°F (190°C).
2. In a large skillet, melt the butter over medium heat. Add the chicken pieces and cook until browned and cooked through. Remove the chicken and set it aside.
3. In the same skillet, add the leeks and garlic, cooking for 5 minutes until softened.
4. Sprinkle flour over the leeks and stir for 1 minute. Slowly pour in the chicken broth and cream, stirring until the mixture thickens.
5. Return the chicken to the skillet and add thyme, salt, and pepper. Stir to combine.
6. Roll out the puff pastry and line a pie dish with it. Pour the chicken and leek mixture into the crust.
7. Cover with the remaining puff pastry, sealing the edges. Brush with the beaten egg.

8. Bake for 30-40 minutes, until the crust is golden and flaky.
9. Serve hot.

# Steak & Ale Pie

Steak & Ale Pie is a classic British dish where tender beef is slow-cooked in ale and served in a flaky pastry crust. The rich flavors of the meat and beer come together to create an incredibly satisfying meal.

Prep Time: 20 minutes Cook Time: 2 hours

## Ingredients:

- 1 pound beef stew meat, cubed
- 2 tablespoons olive oil
- 1 large onion, chopped
- 2 cloves garlic, minced
- 2 cups ale (such as stout or porter)
- 1 cup beef broth
- 1 tablespoon tomato paste
- 1 tablespoon Worcestershire sauce
- 1 teaspoon thyme leaves
- Salt and pepper to taste
- 1 sheet puff pastry
- 1 egg, beaten (for egg wash)

## Method:

1. Preheat the oven to 375°F (190°C).
2. In a large pot, heat olive oil over medium-high heat. Brown the beef stew meat on all sides.
3. Add the onion and garlic, cooking for 5 minutes until softened.
4. Stir in the ale, beef broth, tomato paste, Worcestershire sauce, and thyme. Bring to a simmer.
5. Reduce the heat to low and cook for 1.5-2 hours, until the beef is tender and the sauce has thickened.
6. Season with salt and pepper.
7. Transfer the mixture to a pie dish and top with the puff pastry. Seal the edges and brush with the beaten egg.
8. Bake for 30-35 minutes, until the pastry is golden brown.
9. Serve hot.

# Traditional Fish & Chips

Fish & Chips is a quintessential British dish, known for its crispy battered fish paired with crunchy, golden fries. It's a simple yet delicious comfort food enjoyed by many.

Prep Time: 15 minutes Cook Time: 20 minutes

## Ingredients:

- ✓ 4 white fish fillets (such as cod or haddock)
- ✓ 1 cup all-purpose flour
- ✓ 1 teaspoon baking powder
- ✓ ½ teaspoon salt
- ✓ 1 cup cold beer (or sparkling water)
- ✓ 4 large potatoes, peeled and cut into fries
- ✓ Vegetable oil for frying

## Method:

1. Heat oil in a deep fryer or large pot to 350°F (175°C).
2. In a large bowl, combine the flour, baking powder, and salt. Gradually whisk in the cold beer until the batter is smooth.
3. Dip the fish fillets into the batter, coating them evenly.
4. Carefully lower the fish into the hot oil and fry for 6-8 minutes, until golden and crispy.
5. In a separate pot, fry the potato fries for 5-7 minutes until golden brown and crispy.
6. Serve the fish and chips with tartar sauce and lemon wedges.

# Beer-Battered Cod

Beer-Battered Cod is a crispy, golden fish dish that uses beer in the batter for extra crunch and flavor. It's the perfect pub-style dish to enjoy at home with fries and a cold pint of beer.

Prep Time: 10 minutes  Cook Time: 15 minutes

## Ingredients:

- ✓ 4 cod fillets
- ✓ 1 cup all-purpose flour
- ✓ 1 teaspoon salt
- ✓ 1 teaspoon pepper
- ✓ 1 teaspoon paprika
- ✓ 1 cup beer (preferably a lager)
- ✓ Vegetable oil for frying

## Method:

1. Preheat oil in a deep fryer or large skillet to 350°F (175°C).
2. In a shallow dish, combine flour, salt, pepper, and paprika.
3. Dredge the cod fillets in the flour mixture, ensuring they are well coated.
4. Dip the fillets in the beer, then fry in the hot oil for 5-7 minutes, until golden and crispy.
5. Remove from oil and drain on paper towels.
6. Serve with tartar sauce, fries, or your favorite sides.

# Smoked Haddock Chowder

Smoked Haddock Chowder is a creamy, flavorful soup made with tender smoked haddock, vegetables, and a rich broth. It's the perfect dish to warm you up on a chilly day.

Prep Time: 15 minutes Cook Time: 30 minutes

## Ingredients:

- 1 pound smoked haddock fillets, skin removed
- 1 large onion, chopped
- 2 cloves garlic, minced
- 2 large potatoes, peeled and diced
- 2 cups vegetable or fish broth
- 1 cup heavy cream
- 2 tablespoons butter
- 1 cup frozen peas
- Salt and pepper to taste

## Method:

1. In a large pot, melt butter over medium heat. Add the onion and garlic, cooking until softened, about 5 minutes.
2. Add the potatoes and broth. Bring to a boil, then reduce to a simmer for 15-20 minutes, until the potatoes are tender.
3. Add the smoked haddock and cook for 5-7 minutes until it flakes easily.
4. Stir in the cream and peas. Simmer for an additional 5 minutes.
5. Season with salt and pepper before serving.

# Irish Pork Belly with Apple Sauce

This Irish Pork Belly with Apple Sauce recipe combines tender, crispy pork belly with a sweet and tangy apple sauce. The perfect balance of flavors makes this dish a crowd-pleaser.

Prep Time: 10 minutes Cook Time: 2 hours

## Ingredients:

- ✓ 2 pounds pork belly
- ✓ 1 tablespoon olive oil
- ✓ Salt and pepper to taste
- ✓ 2 apples, peeled, cored, and chopped
- ✓ 1 tablespoon sugar
- ✓ 1 teaspoon cinnamon
- ✓ 1 tablespoon apple cider vinegar

## Method:

1. Preheat the oven to 350°F (175°C).
2. Rub the pork belly with olive oil and season generously with salt and pepper.
3. Roast the pork belly for 2 hours, turning halfway through, until the skin is crispy and the meat is tender.
4. For the apple sauce, combine the apples, sugar, cinnamon, and vinegar in a pot. Cook over medium heat for 15-20 minutes, until the apples are soft.
5. Serve the pork belly slices with a dollop of apple sauce.

# Seafood Pie

Seafood Pie is a comforting dish with a creamy filling made from a variety of seafood, topped with a golden, flaky crust. It's a classic, indulgent meal perfect for seafood lovers.

Prep Time: 20 minutes Cook Time: 45 minutes

## Ingredients:

- ✓ 1 pound mixed seafood (shrimp, scallops, mussels)
- ✓ 1 cup fish stock
- ✓ 1 cup heavy cream
- ✓ 1 tablespoon butter
- ✓ 1 tablespoon flour
- ✓ 1 cup frozen peas
- ✓ 1 sheet puff pastry
- ✓ 1 egg, beaten (for egg wash)
- ✓ Salt and pepper to taste

## Method:

1. Preheat the oven to 375°F (190°C).
2. In a large pot, melt butter over medium heat. Add the flour and cook for 1 minute. Slowly whisk in the fish stock and cream, simmering until thickened.
3. Stir in the seafood and peas, cooking until the seafood is just cooked. Season with salt and pepper.
4. Pour the mixture into a pie dish and cover with puff pastry. Seal the edges and brush with beaten egg.
5. Bake for 35-40 minutes until golden brown.
6. Serve hot.

# Bacon & Cabbage with Parsley Sauce

Bacon & Cabbage with Parsley Sauce is a traditional Irish dish, perfect for celebrating St. Patrick's Day or any occasion. The salty bacon pairs wonderfully with the tender cabbage, while the parsley sauce adds a fresh, herby flavor.

Prep Time: 10 minutes  Cook Time: 30 minutes

## Ingredients:

- ✓ 1 pound bacon (preferably back bacon)
- ✓ 1 medium cabbage, chopped
- ✓ 2 tablespoons butter
- ✓ 2 tablespoons flour
- ✓ 1 cup milk
- ✓ 2 tablespoons fresh parsley, chopped
- ✓ Salt and pepper to taste

## Method:

1. Bring a large pot of salted water to a boil. Add the bacon and simmer for 15-20 minutes until cooked through.
2. Remove the bacon and set aside. In the same pot, add the chopped cabbage and cook for 5-7 minutes, until tender.
3. For the parsley sauce, melt butter in a saucepan over medium heat. Stir in flour and cook for 1 minute. Gradually whisk in the milk, cooking until the sauce thickens.
4. Stir in the parsley, salt, and pepper.
5. Serve the bacon with cabbage, drizzling the parsley sauce on top.

# Colcannon (Mashed Potatoes with Cabbage)

Colcannon is a traditional Irish dish of mashed potatoes combined with cabbage and butter. It's a comforting and hearty side dish, often served during St. Patrick's Day, but perfect for any occasion that calls for a little Irish flair.

Prep Time: 15 minutes Cook Time: 20 minutes

## Ingredients:

- ✓ 2 pounds potatoes, peeled and cubed
- ✓ 1/2 head of cabbage, chopped
- ✓ 4 tablespoons butter, divided
- ✓ 1/2 cup milk
- ✓ Salt and pepper to taste
- ✓ 1/4 cup green onions or scallions, chopped (optional)

## Method:

1. Bring a large pot of salted water to a boil and cook the potatoes for 15 minutes or until tender.
2. While the potatoes are cooking, steam the cabbage for about 5-7 minutes until softened.
3. Drain the potatoes and return them to the pot. Mash the potatoes with half the butter and milk, adding salt and pepper to taste.
4. Stir in the cabbage (and green onions, if using).
5. Serve the colcannon with a dollop of butter on top.

# Champ (Mashed Potatoes with Scallions)

Champ is a classic Irish dish featuring mashed potatoes combined with scallions (green onions). It's a simple, flavorful side dish with a creamy texture, perfect for any Irish meal.

Prep Time: 10 minutes  Cook Time: 20 minutes

## Ingredients:

- ✓ 2 pounds potatoes, peeled and cubed
- ✓ 1 bunch scallions, chopped
- ✓ 4 tablespoons butter, divided
- ✓ 1/2 cup milk
- ✓ Salt and pepper to taste

## Method:

1. Boil the potatoes in salted water for 15 minutes or until soft.
2. While the potatoes cook, heat 2 tablespoons of butter in a small pan. Add the scallions and cook for 2-3 minutes, until softened.
3. Drain the potatoes and return them to the pot. Mash the potatoes, adding milk, butter, salt, and pepper.
4. Stir in the cooked scallions.
5. Serve with additional butter on top.

# Roasted Root Vegetables with Honey & Thyme

This dish combines root vegetables like carrots, parsnips, and sweet potatoes with the sweetness of honey and the fragrance of thyme. Roasted to perfection, it's an easy and flavorful side dish that pairs well with many meals.

Prep Time: 10 minutes Cook Time: 35 minutes

## Ingredients:

- ✓ 2 carrots, peeled and cut into sticks
- ✓ 2 parsnips, peeled and cut into sticks
- ✓ 1 sweet potato, peeled and cubed
- ✓ 2 tablespoons olive oil
- ✓ 1 tablespoon honey
- ✓ 2 teaspoons fresh thyme leaves
- ✓ Salt and pepper to taste

## Method:

1. Preheat the oven to 400°F (200°C).
2. Place the root vegetables on a baking sheet and drizzle with olive oil.
3. Sprinkle with thyme, salt, and pepper, and toss to coat.
4. Roast for 30-35 minutes, tossing halfway through, until the vegetables are golden and tender.
5. Drizzle with honey just before serving.

# Boxty (Irish Potato Pancakes)

Boxty is a traditional Irish potato pancake, crispy on the outside and soft on the inside. It's a versatile dish that can be served as a side or breakfast, often topped with sour cream or smoked salmon.

Prep Time: 15 minutes Cook Time: 10 minutes

## Ingredients:

- 2 large potatoes, grated
- 1 cup all-purpose flour
- 1/2 teaspoon baking powder
- 1/2 teaspoon salt
- 1/4 teaspoon black pepper
- 1 egg
- 1/2 cup milk
- 2 tablespoons butter (for frying)

## Method:

1. Grate the potatoes and squeeze out any excess moisture.
2. In a large bowl, combine the grated potatoes, flour, baking powder, salt, and pepper.
3. In a separate bowl, whisk the egg and milk together, then add to the potato mixture. Stir until combined.
4. Heat the butter in a skillet over medium heat. Spoon spoonfuls of the mixture into the skillet, flattening each into a pancake shape.
5. Cook for 3-4 minutes per side, until golden and crispy.
6. Serve with sour cream, smoked salmon, or your favorite topping.

# Buttered Cabbage

Buttered cabbage is a simple yet flavorful Irish side dish. The cabbage is tender and buttery, making it a perfect accompaniment to any hearty meal, especially those with meat.

Prep Time: 5 minutes Cook Time: 15 minutes

## Ingredients:

- 1/2 head of cabbage, chopped
- 3 tablespoons butter
- Salt and pepper to taste

## Method:

1. Bring a pot of salted water to a boil and cook the cabbage for 10-12 minutes, until tender.
2. Drain the cabbage and return it to the pot.
3. Stir in the butter and season with salt and pepper.
4. Serve immediately.

# Parsnip & Potato Gratin

Parsnip & Potato Gratin is a creamy, cheesy side dish that combines the sweetness of parsnips with the heartiness of potatoes. It's a comforting and elegant dish that's perfect for special occasions or holiday meals.

Prep Time: 15 minutes Cook Time: 1 hour

## Ingredients:

- ✓ 2 large potatoes, peeled and thinly sliced
- ✓ 2 large parsnips, peeled and thinly sliced
- ✓ 2 cups heavy cream
- ✓ 1 cup grated cheddar cheese
- ✓ 2 cloves garlic, minced
- ✓ 1 tablespoon butter
- ✓ Salt and pepper to taste

1. **Method:**
2. Preheat the oven to 375°F (190°C).
3. Grease a baking dish with butter.
4. Layer the sliced potatoes and parsnips in the dish, alternating the layers.
5. In a small saucepan, heat the heavy cream with garlic until warm.
6. Pour the cream over the vegetables and sprinkle with cheese.
7. Cover the dish with foil and bake for 45 minutes.
8. Remove the foil and bake for an additional 15 minutes until golden and bubbly.
9. Let it cool for a few minutes before serving.

# Irish Brown Bread

Irish Brown Bread is a hearty, rustic bread made with whole wheat flour. It's dense, flavorful, and perfect for soaking up soups and stews. This bread is a staple in Irish kitchens and makes a great addition to any meal.

Prep Time: 10 minutes Cook Time: 40 minutes

## Ingredients:

- 2 cups whole wheat flour
- 1 cup all-purpose flour
- 1 teaspoon baking soda
- 1/2 teaspoon salt
- 1 tablespoon sugar
- 1 1/2 cups buttermilk

## Method:

1. Preheat the oven to 375°F (190°C).
2. In a large bowl, combine the flours, baking soda, salt, and sugar.
3. Pour in the buttermilk and stir until a dough forms.
4. Turn the dough out onto a floured surface and shape it into a round loaf.
5. Place the dough on a baking sheet and cut a cross on top of the loaf.
6. Bake for 35-40 minutes until the bread sounds hollow when tapped on the bottom.
7. Let the bread cool before slicing.

# Guinness-Braised Onions

Guinness-Braised Onions are a delicious side dish where onions are slow-cooked in rich Guinness stout. The beer imparts a deep, savory flavor to the onions, making this dish a perfect accompaniment to meats.

Prep Time: 10 minutes Cook Time: 45 minutes

## Ingredients:

- ✓ 2 large onions, sliced
- ✓ 2 tablespoons olive oil
- ✓ 1 cup Guinness stout
- ✓ 1 tablespoon brown sugar
- ✓ 1 tablespoon balsamic vinegar
- ✓ Salt and pepper to taste

## Method:

1. Heat olive oil in a large skillet over medium heat. Add the sliced onions and cook for 10 minutes, stirring frequently, until softened.
2. Add the Guinness, brown sugar, and balsamic vinegar to the onions. Bring to a simmer.
3. Reduce the heat and cook for 30-35 minutes, stirring occasionally, until the onions are caramelized and the sauce has thickened.
4. Season with salt and pepper before serving.

# Traditional Soda Bread

Traditional Irish Soda Bread is a simple and rustic bread made without yeast, using baking soda as a leavening agent. It's dense, slightly tangy, and perfect for serving with butter or alongside soups and stews.

Prep Time: 10 minutes Cook Time: 45 minutes

## Ingredients:

- ✓ 4 cups all-purpose flour
- ✓ 1 teaspoon baking soda
- ✓ 1 teaspoon salt
- ✓ 1 3/4 cups buttermilk

## Method:

1. Preheat the oven to 425°F (220°C).
2. In a large bowl, combine the flour, baking soda, and salt.
3. Slowly add the buttermilk and stir until the dough comes together.
4. Turn the dough out onto a floured surface and knead briefly.
5. Shape the dough into a round loaf and place it on a baking sheet.
6. Cut a cross in the top of the dough and bake for 40-45 minutes, until golden brown.
7. Let the bread cool before slicing.

# Carrot & Parsnip Mash

Carrot & Parsnip Mash is a delightful twist on classic mashed potatoes. The sweetness of carrots and parsnips combines with butter and cream for a rich and flavorful side dish.

Prep Time: 10 minutes  Cook Time: 15 minutes

## Ingredients:

- ✓ 2 carrots, peeled and chopped
- ✓ 2 parsnips, peeled and chopped
- ✓ 1/4 cup heavy cream
- ✓ 2 tablespoons butter
- ✓ Salt and pepper to taste

## Method:

1. Boil the carrots and parsnips in salted water for 15 minutes until tender.
2. Drain and mash the vegetables with butter and cream.
3. Season with salt and pepper.
4. Serve warm.

# Classic Reuben Sandwich

The Classic Reuben Sandwich is an iconic deli sandwich made with corned beef, Swiss cheese, sauerkraut, and Russian dressing, all sandwiched between two slices of rye bread. This hearty, flavorful sandwich is perfect for a satisfying lunch or dinner.

Prep Time: 10 minutes Cook Time: 5 minutes

## Ingredients:

- ✓ 4 slices rye bread
- ✓ 1/2 pound corned beef, thinly sliced
- ✓ 4 slices Swiss cheese
- ✓ 1/4 cup sauerkraut, drained
- ✓ 2 tablespoons Russian dressing
- ✓ 2 tablespoons butter

## Method:

1. Spread the Russian dressing on one side of each slice of bread.
2. Layer the corned beef, Swiss cheese, and sauerkraut on two slices of bread.
3. Top with the remaining slices of bread, dressing side down.
4. Heat a skillet over medium heat and melt the butter.
5. Grill the sandwiches for about 3 minutes per side, pressing them slightly with a spatula, until golden brown and the cheese has melted.
6. Serve warm.

# Irish Breakfast Sandwich

The Irish Breakfast Sandwich is a hearty and flavorful breakfast option that includes some of the best of Irish breakfast staples, such as sausage, bacon, fried egg, and black pudding. Served on a soft roll, it's a meal that will keep you full for hours.

Prep Time: 10 minutes Cook Time: 15 minutes

## Ingredients:

- ✓ 2 soft sandwich rolls
- ✓ 2 Irish sausages
- ✓ 2 slices Irish bacon
- ✓ 2 eggs
- ✓ 2 slices black pudding
- ✓ 1 tablespoon butter
- ✓ Salt and pepper to taste

## Method:

1. Cook the sausages and bacon in a skillet over medium heat until golden and crispy.
2. In the same skillet, cook the black pudding slices until crispy on both sides.
3. In another skillet, fry the eggs to your desired doneness.
4. Split the sandwich rolls and toast lightly.
5. Layer the sausages, bacon, black pudding, and egg on the rolls.
6. Season with salt and pepper and serve immediately.

# Corned Beef & Swiss Melt

The Corned Beef & Swiss Melt is a simple yet delicious sandwich made with tender corned beef, creamy Swiss cheese, and tangy mustard, all melted together between two slices of toasted bread. It's a savory, comforting meal perfect for lunch or dinner.

> Prep Time: 10 minutes Cook Time: 5 minutes

## Ingredients:

- ✓ 4 slices rye or sandwich bread
- ✓ 1/2 pound corned beef, thinly sliced
- ✓ 4 slices Swiss cheese
- ✓ 2 tablespoons Dijon mustard
- ✓ 2 tablespoons butter

## Method:

1. Spread the Dijon mustard on one side of each slice of bread.
2. Layer the corned beef and Swiss cheese on two slices of bread.
3. Top with the remaining slices of bread.
4. Heat a skillet over medium heat and melt the butter.
5. Grill the sandwiches for about 3 minutes per side until the bread is golden brown and the cheese has melted.
6. Serve hot.

# Stout-Marinated Steak Sandwich

This Stout-Marinated Steak Sandwich is full of bold flavors, with marinated steak cooked to perfection and paired with fresh vegetables, all served in a soft baguette. The stout marinade tenderizes the steak and adds a rich, deep flavor to each bite.

Prep Time: 10 minutes  Marinating Time: 1 hour  Cook Time: 10 minutes

## Ingredients:

- ✓ 2 sirloin steaks (6 ounces each)
- ✓ 1/2 cup stout beer
- ✓ 1 tablespoon olive oil
- ✓ 1 tablespoon soy sauce
- ✓ 1 teaspoon Worcestershire sauce
- ✓ 1 garlic clove, minced
- ✓ 1 teaspoon black pepper
- ✓ 2 sandwich baguettes
- ✓ 1/2 red onion, thinly sliced
- ✓ 1 cup arugula
- ✓ 2 tablespoons mayonnaise

## Method:

1. In a bowl, mix the stout, olive oil, soy sauce, Worcestershire sauce, garlic, and black pepper.
2. Place the steaks in a shallow dish and pour the marinade over the top. Marinate for at least 1 hour.
3. Preheat a grill or skillet over medium-high heat. Grill the steaks for 4-5 minutes per side for medium-rare or until your desired doneness.
4. Toast the baguettes slightly and spread mayonnaise on the inside of each one.
5. Thinly slice the steak and layer it inside the baguettes.
6. Add the onions and arugula, then serve immediately.

# Dublin-Style Chicken Club

The Dublin-Style Chicken Club is a delicious sandwich that brings together tender grilled chicken, crispy bacon, fresh lettuce, and a tangy mayo-based sauce, all served in a toasted sandwich roll. A perfect blend of flavors that'll satisfy your taste buds.

Prep Time: 10 minutes Cook Time: 10 minutes

## Ingredients:

- ✓ 2 chicken breasts
- ✓ 4 slices bacon
- ✓ 4 slices tomato
- ✓ 2 sandwich rolls
- ✓ 2 tablespoons mayonnaise
- ✓ 1 tablespoon Dijon mustard
- ✓ 1/4 teaspoon smoked paprika
- ✓ Lettuce leaves
- ✓ Olive oil for grilling

## Method:

1. Season the chicken breasts with salt and pepper, and grill them for about 5 minutes per side until fully cooked.
2. While the chicken is grilling, cook the bacon until crispy in a separate skillet.
3. Mix the mayonnaise, mustard, and paprika in a small bowl.
4. Slice the grilled chicken and sandwich rolls.
5. Assemble the sandwich by spreading the mayonnaise mixture on each side of the bread.
6. Layer the chicken, bacon, tomato, and lettuce on the rolls.
7. Serve immediately.

# Guinness BBQ Pulled Pork Sandwich

The Guinness BBQ Pulled Pork Sandwich is a flavorful and hearty meal made with slow-cooked pulled pork that's been marinated in a Guinness-infused BBQ sauce. Served on a soft bun, this sandwich is packed with rich flavors.

Prep Time: 10 minutes Cook Time: 6 hours (slow cooker)

## Ingredients:

- ✓ 2 pounds pork shoulder
- ✓ 1 cup Guinness beer
- ✓ 1/2 cup BBQ sauce
- ✓ 1/4 cup apple cider vinegar
- ✓ 2 tablespoons brown sugar
- ✓ 1 tablespoon Worcestershire sauce
- ✓ 4 soft sandwich buns
- ✓ Pickles (optional)

## Method:

1. In a slow cooker, combine the Guinness, BBQ sauce, apple cider vinegar, brown sugar, and Worcestershire sauce.
2. Add the pork shoulder, cover, and cook on low for 6 hours or until the pork is tender and easily shreds.
3. Shred the pork with a fork and stir it into the sauce.
4. Toast the sandwich buns lightly, then pile the pulled pork on top.
5. Add pickles if desired and serve immediately.

# Smoked Salmon & Cream Cheese Bagel

This Smoked Salmon & Cream Cheese Bagel is a delicious breakfast or brunch option that combines silky cream cheese with the smoky, salty flavors of smoked salmon. Topped with capers and fresh herbs, this bagel is a true treat.

Prep Time: 5 minutes Cook Time: None

## Ingredients:

- 1 bagel, halved and toasted
- 2 tablespoons cream cheese
- 3 ounces smoked salmon
- 1 tablespoon capers
- 1/4 red onion, thinly sliced
- Fresh dill for garnish

## Method:

1. Spread cream cheese on both halves of the toasted bagel.
2. Top with smoked salmon, red onion slices, and capers.
3. Garnish with fresh dill and serve immediately.

# Battered Fish Wrap with Tartar Sauce

This Battered Fish Wrap with Tartar Sauce is a quick and easy dish that brings together crispy battered fish fillets with creamy tartar sauce, wrapped in a soft tortilla. It's a delightful twist on the classic fish and chips.

Prep Time: 10 minutes  Cook Time: 10 minutes

## Ingredients:

- 2 fish fillets (such as cod or haddock)
- 1 cup flour
- 1/2 teaspoon baking powder
- 1/2 teaspoon salt
- 1/2 cup cold sparkling water
- 2 soft flour tortillas
- 1/4 cup tartar sauce
- Lettuce leaves for garnish

## Method:

1. Mix the flour, baking powder, and salt in a bowl. Slowly add sparkling water and whisk to form a batter.
2. Heat oil in a skillet over medium heat. Dip the fish fillets into the batter and fry until golden brown and crispy, about 4 minutes per side.
3. Place the fish fillets in the tortillas and drizzle with tartar sauce.
4. Garnish with lettuce and roll up the wraps.
5. Serve immediately.

# Irish Cheddar & Apple Grilled Cheese

The Irish Cheddar & Apple Grilled Cheese is a perfect balance of savory and sweet. The sharp Irish cheddar melts beautifully, and the fresh apple slices add a crisp, sweet contrast that makes this sandwich a delightful choice for lunch or a snack.

Prep Time: 5 minutes Cook Time: 5 minutes

## Ingredients:

- ✓ 4 slices white or multigrain bread
- ✓ 4 slices Irish cheddar cheese
- ✓ 1 apple, thinly sliced
- ✓ 2 tablespoons butter

## Method:

1. Butter one side of each slice of bread.
2. Layer the cheddar cheese and apple slices between two slices of bread, with the buttered side facing outward.
3. Heat a skillet over medium heat and grill the sandwich until golden brown and the cheese has melted, about 2-3 minutes per side.
4. Serve hot.

# Black Pudding Breakfast Wrap

This Black Pudding Breakfast Wrap is a hearty and filling breakfast, perfect for those who love savory flavors. The rich black pudding, crispy bacon, and eggs all come together in a warm tortilla for a satisfying meal.

Prep Time: 5 minutes Cook Time: 10 minutes

## Ingredients:

- ✓ 2 tortillas
- ✓ 2 eggs
- ✓ 2 slices black pudding
- ✓ 2 slices bacon
- ✓ 1/4 cup baked beans (optional)
- ✓ Butter or oil for frying

## Method:

1. Fry the black pudding slices and bacon in a skillet until crispy.
2. In another skillet, fry the eggs to your desired doneness.
3. Warm the tortillas in the skillet briefly.
4. Assemble the wraps by layering the black pudding, bacon, eggs, and beans (if using) in the center of the tortilla.
5. Fold the wraps and serve immediately.

# Guinness Chocolate Cake

Guinness Chocolate Cake is a rich, moist, and decadent cake that pairs the deep, malty flavor of Guinness beer with the richness of chocolate. It's perfect for any occasion, and the beer adds a unique depth of flavor that enhances the sweetness of the cake.

Prep Time: 15 minutes Cook Time: 1 hour

## Ingredients:

- 1 cup Guinness beer
- 1/2 cup unsalted butter
- 3/4 cup unsweetened cocoa powder
- 2 cups all-purpose flour
- 2 teaspoons baking soda
- 1/2 teaspoon salt
- 1 cup granulated sugar
- 1 cup brown sugar, packed
- 2 large eggs
- 1 teaspoon vanilla extract
- 2/3 cup sour cream

**For the Frosting:**

- 8 ounces cream cheese, softened
- 1/4 cup unsalted butter, softened
- 3 cups powdered sugar
- 2 tablespoons cocoa powder
- 1 teaspoon vanilla extract

## Method:

1. Preheat your oven to 350°F (175°C). Grease and flour two 9-inch round cake pans.
2. In a saucepan, combine Guinness and butter, heating over medium heat until the butter is melted. Stir in the cocoa powder and set aside.

3. In a large bowl, whisk together flour, baking soda, salt, granulated sugar, and brown sugar.
4. Add the beer and cocoa mixture to the dry ingredients and mix until well combined.
5. In a separate bowl, whisk together eggs, vanilla, and sour cream. Add this to the cake batter and mix until smooth.
6. Divide the batter evenly between the prepared pans and bake for 50-60 minutes, or until a toothpick inserted comes out clean. Let the cakes cool in the pans for 10 minutes before transferring to a wire rack to cool completely.
7. For the frosting: Beat together the cream cheese, butter, powdered sugar, cocoa powder, and vanilla extract until smooth and creamy.
8. Once the cakes are cool, spread frosting on top of one layer, then top with the second layer and frost the entire cake.
9. Serve and enjoy!

# Bailey's Cheesecake

Bailey's Cheesecake is a rich, creamy dessert that combines the smoothness of a classic cheesecake with the indulgent flavor of Bailey's Irish Cream. It's the perfect dessert for those who love a little boozy twist on a traditional favorite.

Prep Time: 20 minutes  Cook Time: 1 hour  Chill Time: 4 hours

## Ingredients:

- 1 1/2 cups graham cracker crumbs
- 1/4 cup unsalted butter, melted
- 2 pounds cream cheese, softened
- 1 cup granulated sugar
- 1 teaspoon vanilla extract
- 1/2 cup Bailey's Irish Cream
- 4 large eggs
- 1/4 cup all-purpose flour
- 1/2 cup sour cream

## Method:

1. Preheat your oven to 325°F (160°C). Grease a 9-inch springform pan.
2. In a small bowl, mix the graham cracker crumbs and melted butter. Press the mixture into the bottom of the prepared pan.
3. In a large bowl, beat the cream cheese and sugar until smooth. Add the vanilla extract and Bailey's Irish Cream, and beat again until combined.
4. Add the eggs one at a time, beating well after each addition. Stir in the flour.
5. Pour the cream cheese mixture over the crust in the pan.
6. Bake for 55-60 minutes, or until the center is set and the edges are lightly browned.
7. Let the cheesecake cool in the pan for 10 minutes, then remove the sides of the springform pan.
8. Refrigerate the cheesecake for at least 4 hours, or overnight.

9. Serve with whipped cream or chocolate shavings, if desired.

# Sticky Toffee Pudding

Sticky Toffee Pudding is a classic British dessert made with a moist sponge cake soaked in a rich, buttery toffee sauce. It's the perfect comfort food, especially when served warm with vanilla ice cream or custard.

Prep Time: 15 minutes Cook Time: 45 minutes

## Ingredients:

- ✓ 1 cup pitted dates, chopped
- ✓ 1 cup boiling water
- ✓ 1 teaspoon baking soda
- ✓ 1/2 cup unsalted butter, softened
- ✓ 3/4 cup packed brown sugar
- ✓ 2 large eggs
- ✓ 1 1/2 cups all-purpose flour
- ✓ 1 teaspoon vanilla extract
- ✓ 1/2 teaspoon baking powder
- ✓ 1/4 teaspoon salt

**For the Toffee Sauce:**

- ✓ 1/2 cup unsalted butter
- ✓ 1 cup heavy cream
- ✓ 1 cup packed brown sugar
- ✓ 1 teaspoon vanilla extract

## Method:

1. Preheat your oven to 350°F (175°C). Grease and flour an 8-inch baking dish.
2. In a small bowl, combine the chopped dates, boiling water, and baking soda. Let it sit for 5-10 minutes until the dates soften.
3. In a separate bowl, cream together the butter and brown sugar until fluffy. Add the eggs one at a time, beating well after each addition.
4. Stir in the flour, vanilla extract, baking powder, and salt. Then, fold in the date mixture until well combined.

5. Pour the batter into the prepared dish and bake for 40-45 minutes, or until a toothpick inserted into the center comes out clean.
6. For the toffee sauce: In a saucepan, melt the butter over medium heat. Stir in the heavy cream, brown sugar, and vanilla. Bring to a simmer, and cook for 5 minutes until thickened.
7. Once the pudding is done, poke holes in the top with a fork and pour half of the toffee sauce over it.
8. Let it sit for a few minutes, then serve warm with the remaining toffee sauce and vanilla ice cream or custard.

# Irish Apple Cake

Irish Apple Cake is a traditional Irish dessert made with tart apples and a light, cinnamon-spiced batter. This cake is perfect for autumn or any time you're craving something comforting and sweet.

Prep Time: 15 minutes Cook Time: 1 hour

## Ingredients:

- 3 cups all-purpose flour
- 2 teaspoons baking powder
- 1 teaspoon ground cinnamon
- 1/2 teaspoon salt
- 1/2 cup unsalted butter, cold and cubed
- 3/4 cup granulated sugar
- 2 large eggs
- 1 teaspoon vanilla extract
- 1/2 cup whole milk
- 4 large apples, peeled, cored, and sliced
- 1/4 cup brown sugar

## Method:

1. Preheat your oven to 350°F (175°C). Grease and flour a 9-inch round cake pan.
2. In a large bowl, whisk together the flour, baking powder, cinnamon, and salt.
3. Cut the cold butter into the flour mixture until it resembles breadcrumbs.
4. Stir in the granulated sugar.
5. In a separate bowl, whisk together the eggs, vanilla, and milk. Add this to the flour mixture and stir until combined.
6. Fold in the apple slices and mix until evenly distributed.
7. Pour the batter into the prepared pan and smooth the top.
8. Sprinkle the brown sugar over the top of the cake.
9. Bake for 50-60 minutes, or until a toothpick inserted into the center comes out clean.

10. Let the cake cool in the pan for 10 minutes, then transfer to a wire rack. Serve warm or at room temperature.

# Whiskey Bread Pudding

Whiskey Bread Pudding is a comforting dessert made with day-old bread soaked in a whiskey-infused custard, baked to golden perfection. It's a wonderful way to use up stale bread and creates a decadent treat.

Prep Time: 10 minutes Cook Time: 45 minutes

## Ingredients:

- 4 cups cubed day-old bread
- 2 cups whole milk
- 3/4 cup heavy cream
- 1/4 cup Irish whiskey
- 1/2 cup granulated sugar
- 3 large eggs
- 1 teaspoon ground cinnamon
- 1/2 teaspoon vanilla extract
- 1/4 teaspoon salt

**For the Whiskey Sauce**:

- 1/2 cup heavy cream
- 1/4 cup Irish whiskey
- 1/4 cup brown sugar
- 2 tablespoons unsalted butter

## Method:

1. Preheat your oven to 350°F (175°C). Grease a 9x9-inch baking dish.
2. In a large bowl, whisk together the milk, heavy cream, whiskey, sugar, eggs, cinnamon, vanilla, and salt.
3. Add the cubed bread to the custard mixture, stirring to ensure all the bread is soaked.
4. Pour the mixture into the prepared dish and bake for 40-45 minutes, or until the custard is set and the top is golden.

5. For the whiskey sauce: In a saucepan, combine the cream, whiskey, brown sugar, and butter. Bring to a simmer over medium heat and cook for 5-7 minutes until thickened.
6. Serve the bread pudding warm with the whiskey sauce drizzled over the top.

# Porter Chocolate Mousse

Porter Chocolate Mousse combines the richness of dark chocolate with the deep, malty flavor of porter beer, creating a luxurious and indulgent dessert. This velvety mousse is perfect for special occasions or a sweet treat after dinner.

Prep Time: 20 minutes Chill Time: 2 hours

## Ingredients:

- ✓ 8 oz dark chocolate (70% cocoa)
- ✓ 1/2 cup porter beer
- ✓ 1 cup heavy cream
- ✓ 1/4 cup powdered sugar
- ✓ 1 teaspoon vanilla extract
- ✓ 2 large eggs, separated
- ✓ 1/4 teaspoon salt

## Method:

1. In a heatproof bowl, melt the dark chocolate with the porter beer over a double boiler, stirring occasionally until smooth.
2. In a separate bowl, whip the heavy cream and powdered sugar until soft peaks form. Set aside.
3. In another bowl, whisk the egg yolks and salt until pale and thick.
4. Gradually fold the melted chocolate mixture into the egg yolk mixture, then fold in the whipped cream and vanilla extract.
5. In a clean bowl, beat the egg whites until stiff peaks form. Gently fold the egg whites into the chocolate mixture.
6. Spoon the mousse into serving cups and refrigerate for at least 2 hours to set.
7. Serve chilled, garnished with chocolate shavings or whipped cream if desired.

# Irish Cream Brownies

These Irish Cream Brownies combine the rich chocolatey goodness of brownies with the smooth, creamy flavor of Irish cream liqueur. The result is a decadent dessert that's perfect for anyone who loves both chocolate and Irish whiskey.

Prep Time: 15 minutes  Cook Time: 30 minutes

## Ingredients:

- 1/2 cup unsalted butter
- 8 oz dark chocolate, chopped
- 1 cup granulated sugar
- 3 large eggs
- 1/4 cup Irish cream liqueur
- 1 teaspoon vanilla extract
- 1/2 cup all-purpose flour
- 1/4 teaspoon salt
- 1/2 cup mini chocolate chips (optional)

## Method:

1. Preheat the oven to 350°F (175°C). Grease a 9x9-inch baking pan and line it with parchment paper.
2. Melt the butter and dark chocolate together in a heatproof bowl over a double boiler, stirring until smooth.
3. Remove from heat and stir in the sugar, eggs, Irish cream liqueur, and vanilla extract until well combined.
4. Add the flour and salt, mixing until just combined. If desired, fold in the mini chocolate chips.
5. Pour the batter into the prepared pan and smooth the top.
6. Bake for 25-30 minutes, or until a toothpick inserted comes out with a few moist crumbs.
7. Let cool completely in the pan before cutting into squares and serving.

# Barmbrack (Irish Fruitcake)

Barmbrack is a traditional Irish fruitcake that's made with a delicious mixture of dried fruit, tea, and warm spices. It's commonly enjoyed with a cup of tea and is especially popular around Halloween, when small tokens are sometimes hidden inside.

Prep Time: 15 minutes Cook Time: 1 hour 10 minutes

## Ingredients:

- 1 1/2 cups mixed dried fruit (raisins, currants, sultanas)
- 1 cup strong black tea
- 1/2 cup brown sugar
- 2 tablespoons unsalted butter, softened
- 1 egg
- 1 1/2 cups all-purpose flour
- 1 teaspoon baking powder
- 1/2 teaspoon ground cinnamon
- 1/4 teaspoon ground nutmeg
- 1/4 teaspoon salt
- 1 tablespoon orange zest (optional)

## Method:

1. Preheat the oven to 350°F (175°C). Grease and line a loaf pan.
2. In a bowl, combine the dried fruit and tea, and let it soak for at least 30 minutes, or overnight if possible.
3. In a separate bowl, cream the butter and brown sugar until light and fluffy.
4. Beat in the egg, then sift in the flour, baking powder, cinnamon, nutmeg, and salt.
5. Add the soaked fruit (along with any excess tea), and fold it into the batter. Stir in the orange zest if using.
6. Pour the mixture into the prepared loaf pan and smooth the top.
7. Bake for 60-70 minutes, or until a skewer inserted into the center comes out clean.

8. Let the Barmbrack cool in the pan before turning it out and slicing to serve.

# Chocolate Stout Truffles

Chocolate Stout Truffles are a decadent treat that blends the richness of dark chocolate with the deep flavor of stout beer. The stout enhances the chocolate, creating a truffle that's both smooth and indulgent.

Prep Time: 10 minutes Chill Time: 2 hours

## Ingredients:

- ✓ 8 oz dark chocolate (70% cocoa), chopped
- ✓ 1/4 cup stout beer (such as Guinness)
- ✓ 1/2 cup heavy cream
- ✓ 1/2 teaspoon vanilla extract
- ✓ Cocoa powder, for rolling

## Method:

1. In a heatproof bowl, combine the dark chocolate and heavy cream.
2. In a small saucepan, bring the stout to a simmer over medium heat, then pour it over the chocolate and cream mixture.
3. Let the mixture sit for a few minutes, then stir until smooth and fully combined.
4. Stir in the vanilla extract.
5. Allow the mixture to cool to room temperature, then refrigerate for at least 2 hours until firm.
6. Once chilled, use a spoon or melon baller to scoop out small amounts of the truffle mixture and roll them into balls.
7. Roll the truffles in cocoa powder and refrigerate again for 30 minutes before serving.

# Shamrock Sugar Cookies

Shamrock Sugar Cookies are a festive treat perfect for St. Patrick's Day. They're shaped like shamrocks and coated in sweet sugar, making them a fun and tasty way to celebrate.

Prep Time: 20 minutes  Cook Time: 8-10 minutes

## Ingredients:

- 2 3/4 cups all-purpose flour
- 1 teaspoon baking powder
- 1/4 teaspoon salt
- 1 cup unsalted butter, softened
- 1 1/2 cups granulated sugar
- 1 large egg
- 1 teaspoon vanilla extract
- Green sugar, for decoration

## Method:

1. Preheat the oven to 350°F (175°C). Line a baking sheet with parchment paper.
2. In a bowl, whisk together the flour, baking powder, and salt.
3. In another bowl, beat the butter and sugar together until light and fluffy.
4. Add the egg and vanilla extract, mixing until combined.
5. Gradually add the dry ingredients to the butter mixture, stirring until a dough forms.
6. Roll the dough out on a floured surface to about 1/4-inch thickness. Use a shamrock-shaped cookie cutter to cut out the cookies.
7. Place the cookies on the prepared baking sheet and sprinkle them with green sugar.
8. Bake for 8-10 minutes, or until the edges are lightly golden.
9. Let the cookies cool on a wire rack before serving.

# Raspberry & White Chocolate Scones

These Raspberry & White Chocolate Scones are a delightful treat, perfect for breakfast or afternoon tea. The sweetness of the white chocolate pairs beautifully with the tartness of fresh raspberries, making them a delicious addition to any occasion.

Prep Time: 15 minutes  Cook Time: 20-25 minutes

## Ingredients:

- 2 cups all-purpose flour
- 1/4 cup granulated sugar
- 1 tablespoon baking powder
- 1/4 teaspoon salt
- 1/2 cup unsalted butter, cold and cubed
- 1/2 cup white chocolate chips
- 1/2 cup fresh raspberries
- 2/3 cup heavy cream
- 1 large egg
- 1 teaspoon vanilla extract
- Extra sugar for sprinkling

## Method:

1. Preheat the oven to 400°F (200°C). Line a baking sheet with parchment paper.
2. In a large bowl, whisk together the flour, sugar, baking powder, and salt.
3. Add the cold, cubed butter and use a pastry cutter or your fingers to work it into the dry ingredients until the mixture resembles coarse crumbs.
4. Gently fold in the white chocolate chips and fresh raspberries.
5. In a small bowl, whisk together the heavy cream, egg, and vanilla extract. Add to the flour mixture and stir until just combined.
6. Turn the dough out onto a floured surface and knead it gently a few times to bring it together. Pat the dough into a disk about 1-inch thick.

7. Cut the dough into 8 wedges and place them on the prepared baking sheet. Sprinkle with a little sugar.
8. Bake for 20-25 minutes, or until the scones are golden brown.
9. Allow the scones to cool slightly before serving.

# Irish Oat Flapjacks

Irish Oat Flapjacks are a hearty, sweet treat made with oats, golden syrup, and butter. These flapjacks are chewy, delicious, and perfect for a quick breakfast or snack.

Prep Time: 10 minutes  Cook Time: 25 minutes

## Ingredients:

- ✓ 2 cups rolled oats
- ✓ 1/2 cup unsalted butter
- ✓ 1/4 cup brown sugar
- ✓ 1/4 cup golden syrup
- ✓ 1/4 teaspoon salt
- ✓ 1/2 teaspoon vanilla extract

## Method:

1. Preheat the oven to 350°F (175°C). Grease and line a 9x9-inch baking pan.
2. In a saucepan over medium heat, melt the butter, brown sugar, and golden syrup together until smooth.
3. Stir in the salt and vanilla extract.
4. In a large bowl, combine the rolled oats with the wet mixture and stir until the oats are fully coated.
5. Pour the mixture into the prepared baking pan and press it down firmly.
6. Bake for 25 minutes, or until the flapjacks are golden brown and firm to the touch.
7. Allow to cool in the pan before cutting into squares and serving.

# Bailey's Tiramisu

This Bailey's Tiramisu combines the rich, creamy layers of traditional tiramisu with the smooth, velvety flavor of Bailey's Irish Cream. It's a decadent twist on a classic dessert, perfect for any celebration.

Prep Time: 20 minutes    Chill Time: 4 hours

## Ingredients:

- 1 1/2 cups heavy cream
- 1/2 cup Bailey's Irish Cream
- 8 oz mascarpone cheese, softened
- 1/2 cup powdered sugar
- 1 teaspoon vanilla extract
- 1 cup strong brewed coffee, cooled
- 24 ladyfingers
- Cocoa powder, for dusting

## Method:

1. In a large bowl, beat the heavy cream until stiff peaks form.
2. In a separate bowl, whisk together the mascarpone cheese, powdered sugar, and vanilla extract until smooth.
3. Gently fold the whipped cream and Bailey's Irish Cream into the mascarpone mixture until combined.
4. In a shallow dish, pour the cooled coffee. Quickly dip the ladyfingers into the coffee and layer them in the bottom of a 9x9-inch dish.
5. Spread half of the mascarpone mixture over the ladyfingers. Repeat with another layer of dipped ladyfingers and the remaining mascarpone mixture.
6. Cover and refrigerate for at least 4 hours, or overnight, to allow the flavors to meld.
7. Before serving, dust the top with cocoa powder.

# Irish Whiskey Caramel Tart

This Irish Whiskey Caramel Tart is a showstopper dessert that pairs the rich flavor of whiskey with smooth caramel. The tart's buttery crust complements the sweet, boozy filling perfectly, making it a great choice for special occasions.

Prep Time: 25 minutes Cook Time: 35 minutes

## Ingredients:

- ✓ 1 pre-made tart shell (9-inch)
- ✓ 1 cup heavy cream
- ✓ 1/2 cup granulated sugar
- ✓ 1/4 cup Irish whiskey
- ✓ 1/4 cup unsalted butter
- ✓ 1 teaspoon vanilla extract
- ✓ Pinch of sea salt

## Method:

1. Preheat the oven to 350°F (175°C). Bake the tart shell according to the package instructions until golden brown, then set aside to cool.
2. In a saucepan over medium heat, combine the heavy cream and sugar. Stir until the sugar dissolves and the cream starts to simmer.
3. Remove from heat and stir in the butter, vanilla extract, and Irish whiskey.
4. Return to low heat and cook for 5-7 minutes, stirring constantly, until the caramel thickens.
5. Pour the caramel filling into the cooled tart shell and smooth the top.
6. Refrigerate for at least 2 hours to allow the caramel to set.
7. Before serving, sprinkle with a pinch of sea salt.

# Honey & Oat Ice Cream

This Honey & Oat Ice Cream is a creamy, naturally sweet treat. The combination of honey and oats creates a comforting flavor that's both decadent and wholesome. It's the perfect dessert for summer or anytime you crave something cool and sweet.

Prep Time: 10 minutes Chill Time: 4 hours

## Ingredients:

- 1 1/2 cups heavy cream
- 1 cup whole milk
- 1/2 cup honey
- 1/2 cup rolled oats
- 1 teaspoon vanilla extract

## Method:

1. In a saucepan, heat the milk and honey over medium heat, stirring until the honey dissolves.
2. Remove from heat and stir in the vanilla extract.
3. In a separate bowl, whip the heavy cream until stiff peaks form.
4. Gently fold the whipped cream into the honey and milk mixture.
5. Stir in the rolled oats.
6. Pour the mixture into an ice cream maker and churn according to the manufacturer's instructions.
7. Once churned, transfer to a container and freeze for at least 4 hours or until firm.
8. Serve and enjoy!

# Butterscotch & Stout Pudding

Butterscotch & Stout Pudding is a rich and indulgent dessert that combines the deep flavors of stout beer and butterscotch to create a decadent treat. The creamy, velvety pudding is a perfect ending to any meal.

Prep Time: 10 minutes Cook Time: 15 minutes

## Ingredients:

- 1/2 cup heavy cream
- 1/2 cup stout beer
- 1/2 cup brown sugar
- 1 tablespoon cornstarch
- 1/2 teaspoon vanilla extract
- Pinch of salt

## Method:

1. In a saucepan, combine the heavy cream, stout beer, and brown sugar. Heat over medium heat, stirring until the sugar dissolves.
2. In a small bowl, mix the cornstarch with 2 tablespoons of cold water to form a slurry.
3. Stir the slurry into the stout mixture and cook, stirring constantly, until the pudding thickens.
4. Remove from heat and stir in the vanilla extract and salt.
5. Pour the pudding into serving dishes and refrigerate for at least 2 hours to set.
6. Serve chilled, topped with whipped cream or caramel sauce if desired.

# Irish Coffee Cake

This Irish Coffee Cake is a rich, moist cake flavored with strong coffee and Irish whiskey. Perfect for a morning treat or an afternoon snack, this cake combines the deep, warm flavors of coffee and whiskey, making it a deliciously unique dessert.

Prep Time: 20 minutes Cook Time: 45 minutes

## Ingredients:

- 2 cups all-purpose flour
- 1 1/2 teaspoons baking powder
- 1/2 teaspoon baking soda
- 1/4 teaspoon salt
- 1/2 cup unsalted butter, softened
- 1 cup granulated sugar
- 2 large eggs
- 1/2 cup sour cream
- 1/2 cup brewed strong coffee, cooled
- 1/4 cup Irish whiskey
- 1 teaspoon vanilla extract
- 1/2 cup chopped walnuts or pecans (optional)
- 1 tablespoon brown sugar (for topping)

## Method:

1. Preheat the oven to 350°F (175°C). Grease and flour a 9-inch round cake pan.
2. In a medium bowl, whisk together the flour, baking powder, baking soda, and salt.
3. In a large bowl, beat the butter and sugar together until light and fluffy.
4. Add the eggs, one at a time, beating well after each addition.
5. Stir in the sour cream, brewed coffee, Irish whiskey, and vanilla extract.
6. Gradually add the dry ingredients, mixing until just combined.
7. If using, fold in the chopped walnuts or pecans.

8. Pour the batter into the prepared cake pan and sprinkle the top with brown sugar.
9. Bake for 40-45 minutes, or until a toothpick inserted into the center comes out clean.
10. Allow to cool in the pan for 10 minutes, then transfer to a wire rack to cool completely before serving.

# Whiskey Chocolate Fudge

Whiskey Chocolate Fudge is a decadent dessert combining rich, smooth chocolate with the depth of Irish whiskey. It's a perfect treat for special occasions or when you want a little indulgence with a kick of whiskey.

Prep Time: 15 minutes  Cook Time: 10 minutes  Chill Time: 2 hours

### Ingredients:

- 1 1/2 cups heavy cream
- 2 tablespoons unsalted butter
- 1/2 cup Irish whiskey
- 3 cups semi-sweet chocolate chips
- 1/4 cup granulated sugar
- 1 teaspoon vanilla extract
- Pinch of salt

### Method:

1. Line a 9x9-inch baking pan with parchment paper.
2. In a saucepan over medium heat, combine the heavy cream, butter, and Irish whiskey. Stir occasionally until the mixture begins to simmer.
3. Add the sugar and continue to stir until the sugar is fully dissolved.
4. Remove from heat and stir in the chocolate chips until they are completely melted and the mixture is smooth.
5. Stir in the vanilla extract and a pinch of salt.
6. Pour the fudge mixture into the prepared baking pan and spread it evenly.
7. Refrigerate for at least 2 hours, or until firm.
8. Once set, cut the fudge into small squares and serve.

# Guinness Float

A Guinness Float is a fun and refreshing adult dessert drink that combines the rich flavors of Guinness stout with the creamy goodness of vanilla ice cream. It's a delightful twist on the traditional root beer float, perfect for St. Patrick's Day or any occasion.

Prep Time: 5 minutes  Servings: 1

## Ingredients:

- ✓ 1 bottle of Guinness stout (or any preferred stout)
- ✓ 2 scoops vanilla ice cream
- ✓ Whipped cream (optional)
- ✓ Chocolate shavings or cocoa powder (optional)

## Method:

1. In a tall glass, add two generous scoops of vanilla ice cream.
2. Slowly pour the Guinness stout over the ice cream, allowing it to fizz and settle as you pour.
3. Top with whipped cream, if desired, and garnish with chocolate shavings or a light dusting of cocoa powder.
4. Serve immediately with a spoon and straw.

# Classic Irish Coffee

A Classic Irish Coffee combines the warmth of strong coffee with the richness of Irish whiskey and a layer of lightly whipped cream. It's the perfect drink to enjoy after a meal or on a cozy evening, with just the right balance of sweetness and warmth.

Prep Time: 5 minutes  Servings: 1

## Ingredients:

- ✓ 1 cup freshly brewed hot coffee
- ✓ 1 1/2 ounces Irish whiskey
- ✓ 1 teaspoon brown sugar
- ✓ Heavy cream, lightly whipped

## Method:

1. Brew a cup of your favorite strong coffee.
2. Pour the coffee into a heat-resistant glass or mug.
3. Stir in the brown sugar until fully dissolved.
4. Add the Irish whiskey and stir to combine.
5. Gently float a layer of lightly whipped cream on top by pouring it over the back of a spoon.
6. Serve immediately and enjoy!

# Bailey's Irish Cream Latte

The Bailey's Irish Cream Latte is a delightful twist on the classic latte, combining the smoothness of coffee with the indulgent flavor of Bailey's Irish Cream. This warm, creamy drink is perfect for a cozy winter morning or as an after-dinner treat.

Prep Time: 5 minutes

## Ingredients:

- 1 shot of espresso (or 1/2 cup strong brewed coffee)
- 1 ounce Bailey's Irish Cream
- 1/2 cup steamed milk
- Whipped cream (optional)
- Cocoa powder or cinnamon for garnish (optional)

## Method:

1. Brew a shot of espresso or prepare strong coffee.
2. Steam your milk until frothy (you can use a milk frother or heat it on the stove).
3. In a large mug, combine the espresso and Bailey's Irish Cream.
4. Pour the steamed milk over the espresso and Bailey's mixture.
5. Stir gently to combine.
6. Top with whipped cream and a sprinkle of cocoa powder or cinnamon, if desired.
7. Serve and enjoy!

# Guinness & Blackcurrant

Guinness & Blackcurrant is a refreshing and unique drink made by combining the deep flavors of Guinness stout with the fruity tang of blackcurrant cordial. It's a popular drink in Ireland, offering a smooth and slightly sweet contrast to the richness of the stout.

| Prep Time: 5 minutes |
| --- |

## Ingredients:

- ✓ 1 bottle Guinness stout
- ✓ 1 ounce blackcurrant cordial (like Ribena)
- ✓ Ice (optional)

## Method:

1. Pour the Guinness stout into a pint glass, filling it about three-quarters full.
2. Slowly add the blackcurrant cordial.
3. Stir gently to combine.
4. If desired, add a few ice cubes to chill the drink.
5. Serve immediately.

# Irish Mule (Whiskey & Ginger Beer)

The Irish Mule is a delightful variation of the classic Moscow Mule, featuring Irish whiskey instead of vodka. With its refreshing combination of ginger beer and lime, this drink is perfect for anyone who loves whiskey and refreshing cocktails.

Prep Time: 5 minutes

## Ingredients:

- 2 ounces Irish whiskey
- 4 ounces ginger beer
- 1/2 ounce fresh lime juice
- Lime wedge for garnish
- Mint leaves for garnish (optional)

## Method:

1. Fill a mule mug (or a highball glass) with ice.
2. Pour the Irish whiskey and lime juice over the ice.
3. Top with ginger beer and stir gently.
4. Garnish with a lime wedge and mint leaves, if desired.
5. Serve immediately.

# Black Velvet (Guinness & Champagne)

A Black Velvet is a sophisticated cocktail that combines the richness of Guinness with the effervescence of champagne. It's perfect for celebrations or for anyone looking for a unique and elegant drink.

Prep Time: 5 minutes

## Ingredients:

- 1/2 glass Guinness stout
- 1/2 glass chilled champagne

## Method:

1. Pour the Guinness stout into a flute or champagne glass, filling it halfway.
2. Slowly top with chilled champagne.
3. Stir gently to combine.
4. Serve immediately.

# Dublin Sour (Whiskey & Lemon)

The Dublin Sour is a variation of the classic whiskey sour, made with Irish whiskey and fresh lemon juice. It's a tangy and refreshing drink with a smooth finish, ideal for those who enjoy whiskey-based cocktails.

Prep Time: 5 minutes

## Ingredients:

- ✓ 2 ounces Irish whiskey
- ✓ 1 ounce fresh lemon juice
- ✓ 3/4 ounce simple syrup
- ✓ Ice
- ✓ Lemon twist or cherry for garnish

## Method:

1. In a cocktail shaker, combine the Irish whiskey, lemon juice, and simple syrup.
2. Fill the shaker with ice and shake vigorously for about 15 seconds.
3. Strain into a chilled cocktail glass.
4. Garnish with a lemon twist or a cherry.
5. Serve immediately.

# Shamrock Shake (Alcoholic or Non-Alcoholic)

The Shamrock Shake is a fun, minty milkshake that's perfect for St. Patrick's Day. Whether you choose to make it alcoholic or non-alcoholic, it's a creamy and refreshing treat for all ages.

Prep Time: 5 minutes

## Ingredients:

- 2 cups vanilla ice cream
- 1/2 cup milk
- 1/2 teaspoon mint extract
- 1/4 teaspoon vanilla extract
- 2 ounces Irish whiskey (optional for alcoholic version)
- Green food coloring (optional)
- Whipped cream for garnish

## Method:

1. In a blender, combine the vanilla ice cream, milk, mint extract, vanilla extract, and Irish whiskey (if using).
2. Blend until smooth.
3. Add a few drops of green food coloring, if desired, and blend again.
4. Pour into a glass and top with whipped cream.
5. Serve immediately.

# Bailey's Espresso Martini

The Bailey's Espresso Martini combines the richness of coffee, the smoothness of Bailey's Irish Cream, and the kick of vodka, creating a perfect cocktail for coffee lovers. This drink is ideal as an after-dinner indulgence.

Prep Time: 5 minutes

## Ingredients:

- ✓ 1 ounce Bailey's Irish Cream
- ✓ 1 ounce vodka
- ✓ 1 ounce freshly brewed espresso (cooled)
- ✓ Ice
- ✓ Coffee beans for garnish (optional)

## Method:

1. In a cocktail shaker, combine the Bailey's Irish Cream, vodka, and cooled espresso.
2. Fill the shaker with ice and shake vigorously for 15-20 seconds.
3. Strain into a chilled martini glass.
4. Garnish with coffee beans, if desired.
5. Serve immediately.

# Irish Hot Toddy

An Irish Hot Toddy is the perfect warming drink for a chilly evening. Made with Irish whiskey, honey, and lemon, it's a comforting drink that helps you unwind and relax.

Prep Time: 5 minutes

## Ingredients:

- ✓ 2 ounces Irish whiskey
- ✓ 1 tablespoon honey
- ✓ 1 tablespoon fresh lemon juice
- ✓ Hot water
- ✓ Lemon slice and cinnamon stick for garnish

## Method:

1. In a mug, combine the Irish whiskey, honey, and lemon juice.
2. Fill the mug with hot water and stir until the honey dissolves.
3. Garnish with a slice of lemon and a cinnamon stick.
4. Serve immediately.

# Stout & Irish Cream Milkshake

The Stout & Irish Cream Milkshake is a rich and creamy treat for those who love the combination of stout beer and Irish cream. This milkshake is perfect for a decadent dessert or an indulgent treat.

Prep Time: 5 minutes

## Ingredients:

- 1/2 cup Guinness stout
- 2 scoops vanilla ice cream
- 1 ounce Bailey's Irish Cream
- Whipped cream for topping
- Chocolate shavings (optional)

## Method:

1. In a blender, combine the Guinness stout, vanilla ice cream, and Bailey's Irish Cream.
2. Blend until smooth and creamy.
3. Pour into a tall glass and top with whipped cream.
4. Garnish with chocolate shavings, if desired.
5. Serve immediately.

# Green Beer

Green Beer is a fun and festive drink, especially popular on St. Patrick's Day. It's simply beer with a touch of food coloring to make it a vibrant green, adding a fun twist to your usual pint.

| Prep Time: 1 minute |
| --- |

## Ingredients:

- 1 pint of beer (lager or pale ale works best)
- Green food coloring

## Method:

1. Pour the beer into a pint glass.
2. Add a drop or two of green food coloring into the beer.
3. Stir gently to combine.
4. Serve immediately.